DEDICATION

I would like to dedicate this Book to my
wife Sherolyn Dyer,
all of our six children, and to
The Body of Christ World Wide.

I want to thank all the Saints who have spoken
prophetic WORDS over me, for without your in
put this would perhaps never came to fruition.

I also want to thank my Pastor for his steadfastness to allow me
to speak to his sheep, and he really watches out for his flock.

Jesus said, " Thus the last will be first and the first last."
This is exactly how I was put on this journey with the
Holy Spirit getting ALL the credit. He is The One
that taught me all that is within these pages.

The FIRST thing He spoke to me was, to go and set
His People FREE. My instant response was,
"I can't do that! He said you answered correctly,
but I can through you, and I agreed.

There is only one way FREEDOM comes in
The Kingdom of God and that is Knowing the TRUTH.

Jesus said in John 8:32 And you shall know the truth: and
the truth, - (that **YOU** Know) - shall make you free.

Now nearing the end of my journey, here on planet
earth comes the completion of what He said back in
December 10, 1984 @ 3:17 AM –
Go and set my people FREE.

My only desire is that The Body of Christ will be
made free from what the Holy Spirit has Revealed.

**"Lord we All await
Your Return"**

Choose a really good prayer partner

Table of contents.

**The Second Coming of Jesus Christ
As Revealed by THE FATHER**

By Ronald Dyer

What are some of the reasons why one should read this book?

Please let me mention a few: ~~~

1) The information between these pages will reveal where **YOU** came from.

2) You will be shown the Dilemma that **YOU** were born into.

3) YOU will be given the opportunity to change where **YOU** will spend Eternity.

4) Heaven IS a Choice; it is a free gift called GRACE, **YOU** are Responsible to choose.

5) YOU and Jesus have The Same FATHER.

> **A) You** used to walk on streets of Gold, but **You** were removed from that place.
>
> **B) YOUR** Earthly spiritual father came from Heaven, but he has another name.
>
> **C)** Jesus wants to reveal to **YOU** Who His Father is.
>
> **D)** The Father wants to Reveal to **YOU**, How **YOU** can be Certain of His Son's return.

10 ~ Reasons to write this book.

1. ~ Dec. 10,1984 - After studying till about 3:00 a.m. I went to the bathroom before retiring; and at 3:17 a.m. the Lord spoke to me and said, "**Set my people free**", I said, "Lord, I can't do that", He said, "No, you can't, but **I can through you**"; and **I agreed**.

When I came out of the bathroom my wife said, that I looked pale as a ghost. That was only the second time that I remember that God' had spoken to me. Did I understand what the implications of that were? No, all I knew was that if He said it, it would have be up to Him to bring it to pass.

After taking a personality profile test at church, I began to get a CLUE! My results showed that I had the profile that matched **ABRAHAM**, and **MOSES.**

Jesus said, "**Y**ou **S**hall **K**now **T**he **T**ruth and the truth **YOU KNOW** will **MAKE YOU FREE**". Freedom comes by knowing **WHO** you are by **SPIRIT**. Jesus also said, in ~

Zec 4:6 *'Your help __will not come__ from __your own strength__ and power. No, your __help will come__ from __my Spirit__.' This is what the LORD All-Powerful says.* **(ERV)**

2. ~ Dec. 10, 1984 - During that same Sunday morning service Sister B. called me out into the isle an said, "The lord is anointing you with the **same anointing** that He **gave Aaron**, and she said, she could see that anointing **oil** running down over my head and down through my beard, then she said, the Lord was anointing my hands with healing".

Exo 4:16 *So Aaron will speak for you. Like God, you will speak to him, and he will tell the people what you say.* **(ERV)**

I was totally taken by surprise when "**Sister B**" called me

out into the center of the isle and started prophesying over me.

Yet my spirit man was quiet and ready to receive the things of God.

One day Years Ago, I was having A BAD DAY;I mean REALLY bad ~~~ (Explanation of that day should be another book) ~~~ I was on my job eating lunch feeling down and I heard these words ~ "**Look Up"**. When I looked up I was looking at an old delivery truck ~ junked ~ and on the side of the truck was this WORD. AA**RON** all in capitol letters, and The Lord encouraged my by saying, "I had YOU in mind WHEN I Named Aaron ~ I included your name in his **(RON).** His peace came immediately, then I chose to enter into His Rest".

3. ~ Dec. 10, 1984 ~ At that evening service she called me out again and said, "The Lord is **anointing you** with the ability to **speak things into existence**".

The whole congregation was encouraged to come back
for the Sunday Evening Service and we did. She said, "That God
told her that He was going to release The Anointing to Speak thing
into existence! ~~~ My thought was that **ALL** would probably receive this gift
from God, Right. To my Great Surprise, I was the only one she called out
to receive this impartation.

In order to speak anything into existence, it can only be done by and
through His Anointing and calling. The **TRUTH** that will make
us free is to know **by SPIRIT** Who we are **in Christ.**

1Jn 4:17 *If God's love is made perfect in us, we can be __without fear__ on the __day__ when God __judges the world__. We will __be without fear__, because __in this world__ we __are like Jesus__.* **(ERV)**

4. ~ **Mar - 88**   Nora Lam called us out of 253 people that night and said that, "there was a **call of God** on our lives," because she said that the Holy Spirit showed her that there was a **Halo of Light** over both of us. ~ "She said that," God was going to use me mightily".

> **Rom 11:29** *God never changes his mind about the people he calls.*
> *He never decides to take back the blessings he has given them.* **(ERV)**

> **Eph 4:8** *Wherefore he saith, When he **ascended** up on high,*
> *he **led captivity captive**, and gave **gifts unto men**.* **(KJV)**

> **The Truth is that whatever you have been given to do in**
> **His Kingdom, was given to You through His ascension Gifts to men.**

> **Php 2:13** *For it is **God who is producing in you** both*
> *the **desire and the ability** to do what pleases him.* **(ISV)**

5. ~ **Dec. 7, 1990** It was prophesied over me that, "I should speak forth **The Oracles of God**".

> **Mat 24:45** *Who are faithful and wise servants?*
> *Who are the ones the master will put in charge of giving*
> *the other servants **their food supplies** at the **proper time**?* **(CEV)**

6. ~ This is a quote from a Prophet by the name of Myrid Sprigler on Dec 6, 1990, "The Lord says, "I haven't called you to travel along behind, I've called you to be a leader, I've Called You to be My man." The Lord says, "I'm going to **teach** you some things about submission; I'm going to teach you some things about **the Word** of God. The Lord says, "you know a lot of things, but you're not really hearing clearly **what the Spirit is saying** to the church; and, "I'll make you a man of the spirit; and the lord says, "I'll make you a man of The Spirit, as new power is going to come; there will be a new release come; there's going to be a whole **New Avenue** that **God's** going **to open up for you**. It's almost like God says, "I'm going to give You **your own Avenue** to walk down"; The Lord says, "I want you to submit to my leading and my guidance and **let me** take you on **into** the things of God". Amen. God's Faithful.

I had been faithfully studying God's Word for seven years and had seen zero fruit ~

I had asked my pastor about this situation and he said; I don't know what you have, but whatever it is ,it has to come from God because no natural man would have done the work you had done for the past seven years without God being The Source.

He then advised me to just lay it down, if God is in it, HE will see to it that You Take it up again. For the next six months I didn't study ,I didn't read my bible or anything. I felt like I had wasted seven years of my life for NOTHING. After this six months period of time God sent these two prophets that set me back on coarse. God IS <u>VERY GOOD</u>.

7. ~ Prophet Tim Meyers spoke next saying, "Father we <u>**just call in the finances and the**</u> <u>**heart**</u>,~~~ father the heart, we thank you for the **wisdom** to develop all these things, and the **understanding** of how he's supposed to **apply all these things**, and Father we just call forth <u>that anointing</u> right now in the name of Jesus.

This was the most <u>**RE-ASSURING**</u> thing that had happened to me till that time. My Spirit man bore witness with this ***message that was coming from Heaven*** through this man. What is the saying, ~~~ "**<u>All</u>** my confusion **HE UNDERSTOOD**" That night God fused into me everything that He had revealed to me by His Spirit, That night I knew that God wanted me to continue on the path that **He HAD** set me on.

God's **<u>WORD</u>** is not only **<u>TRUTH</u>** it is also **<u>PROFOUND TRUTH</u>**.

Php 2:13 *Yes, it is God who is working in you. He helps you want to do what pleases him, and he gives you the power to do it.* **(ERV)**

8. ~ On April 26, 2008 a man prayed over me and said, "He is a **<u>Son of Zadox</u>**"; and The **<u>staff</u>** was coming **to Lead**.

9. ~ The name **<u>DYER</u>** goes all the way back to ~~~ (**Exodus 25:5** *And rams' skins **<u>dyed</u>** red, and badgers' skins, and shittim wood,* **(KJV)** ~ we were the **"<u>dyers</u>"** of the cloth.

In December of 1985 about 10:00 o'clock one evening I was studying "The **<u>Word</u>**"; and ***was caught up to Heaven*** for a few minutes. I first saw a real large gathering of people and I was up in a balcony type area over looking the proceedings and Jesus was standing on an elevated platform so all could see Him. He was speaking to this very large gathering of people. The next thing I remember, I was in a smaller area with Jesus and was looking down towards Earth. I was watching myriad's of people leaving heaven for planet Earth. As I was watching all these people going to Earth; Jesus said to me, "You haven't left yet? I responded to him by saying, "I don't know if I will make it back? As I turned to Him, He responded with a smile, "You'll make it back."

As I reflect back on my experience, I am firmly convinced of what I saw. Jesus was showing me the results of what one third of the angels refused to do. The command of God was to worship "**The image of God**"; whom He had named ~ **(ADAM)** ~. Then the following scene I saw one third of the angels being cast out of Heaven ~~~ **Rev 12:9** *And the great dragon was cast out, that old serpent, called the Devil, and Satan, which deceiveth the whole world: he was **cast out into the earth**, and **his angels** were **cast out with him**.* **(KJV)**

After I was back in this present world, I can reflect on how I felt. I now remember of being in a state of fuzziness; like what was I doing? I remember thinking I was reading the bible; but not sure exactly where or what I was doing. I looked down at my bible and the very first verse I saw was ~

Mat 24:45 *"Who then is a faithful and wise servant, whom his master appointed over his household, to give them food in due season?* **(EMTV)**

The Holy Spirit softly spoke to me, that's WHO You Are!
The same as was written about Mary, she pondered these things
in her heart. That's all you can do until more confirmation comes.

10. ~ Ron Dyer Dream: I had a dream on Sept 2, 2015 to this effect.

I had a dream that I was going back to do some carpentry at a house that I had worked on many times before, and I was considered as family to these people. Before I started to work I had to use the bathroom. Knowing where the three of them were I proceeded to the nearest one which was the master bedroom.

I went straight to the master bedroom and looked all around and behold there was no bathroom. I proceeded to the next bathroom and there I found the flush; but it had been altered to something I had never seen before. Looked like a normal flush but after investigating I looked at the drain, but there was no drain. When I looked into the flush there was no drain in it, the bottom was a half round tank with no drain.

I then proceeded to the third bathroom, looked all around and could not see the flush. I found where it was supposed to be, but it wasn't there. I was slightly bewildered by all of this, finally I was drawn to the bathroom window, but the bathroom window wasn't even in the same place. The bathroom window was near the ceiling and then I saw the flush was connected to the window.

I finally got elevated to the height of the flush connected to this window, as I sat on the flush I could see the view of a large city in the background though the house was located in the country.

~~~~~~

God gives me the interpretation on **Sept 14, 2015 @ 1:25 am** while I am sitting on my flush, doing what I had to do on the flush in the dream.

This is what I received:

He said what I have called you to deliver could not be received in the first Room you visited, it went nowhere ~~~ (That Church no longer exists.) You entered the second room, there was a place to deliver my message but it would only be contained in that house, that is why there was no drain and it would only remain in that house.

The last room was the appointed room, the message I gave you to deliver did not come from your natural mind; that is why the delivery point was not in the normal place. My message comes from a higher place, that is why you had to look up to find it. My message through you is not meant to be contained in just one house.

My message through you is intended for the whole world that is why I showed you the flush in the window, because the message I have given you is for the whole World.

The struggles, trials, and difficulties to fulfill your calling!!!

I guess the best place to start is "In The Beginning", correct! I was born July 27, 1943 in Augusta General Hospital in Augusta, Maine, to Herbert and Mava Dyer. I was told that I had to stay in the hospital for 4-6 weeks because my total body was covered with boils. My mother told me that it was a sad sight and just awful. This was not a good beginning.

I went to a one room school house in 1948 and had my first bad experience. I can't remember if I was 6 or 7 at the time of the episode. I remember walking toward the one room school house when all of a sudden someone pushed me really hard in the back, it at least knocked the wind out of me. That was all I remembered at the time, then many years later the one who pushed me down, asked me if I remembered the time that I almost didn't make it through grammar school? I asked what do you mean? He said, do you remember the day that I shoved you to the ground really hard? I said, yes I remember the experience your referring to.

Then he explains to me what happened. He said you were walking towards the school house not aware that another student was running really fast towards you with his fathers hunting knife held high over his head, ready to knife you in the back; it was then I saw you were in danger, I ran and knocked to out of the way of the knife. ~~~ **God's provision and intervention!!**

Growing up I nearly drowned several times, had a rollover with an automobile, a close brush with death at a cedar mill ~~~ hit in the chin with a fast flying board from a stripper saw that knocked me down. I destroyed my snowmobile, and ended up in the hospital. In 1999 I had a cardiomyopathy ~~ (heart attack) ~~ my heart was only pumping out 20% of the blood instead of the normal 85%. I had a house trailer fall on me and all that were there thought I was dead. All together I have had 13 near death experiences.

The last one was, that I hope and pray I "**NEVER**" have to repeat. It was by far the scariest thing I've experienced. This is what happened:

I was working on a project that was reclaiming 10 acres of the Kennebec River for a Land Level Transfer Station for Naval Vessels. This project required that we were continually working over the water. In late November of 1999 ~ (cold) ~ I was asked to get some chipping bits for a small jack hammer. After getting all the bits ~ (8 of them) about 25-30 lbs. I had to climb back down to the water level with these bits in my right arm. While stepping down from one level to the next I slipped and fell onto concrete, hit my head which knocked me unconscious: ~~~

When I came too again, I was about 30 feet down in the river looking up! ~~ there was a huge barge to my left, I was hoping that I wouldn't get taken under the barge by the current in the river!!! To the right of the barge all I could see was a light the size of a quarter, which was getting **SMALLER** by the second.. ~~~ I wasn't a ware that I still had a hold of the 30 lbs. of bits that were taking me to the bottom of the 100 ft. deep river. ~~~ The next thing I do is to start heading for that light with all my might.

When I finally get to the top of the river ~ there is one final challenge. I need someone to pull me out of the river, without help there would be no way for me to get out. ~~~ Here's the problem: There are more than 20 diesel engines running on all kinds of equipment, making a lot of noise. I holler but no one can hear me, plus no one knows that I'm **IN The River**!

"BUT" ~ **THE FAITHFUL ONE**, that started a good work in me, ~ who also said, ~ that He would complete it, came through. ~~~ God's provision came to pass when my partner came looking for me, as we were required to know that the person we were working with was safe at all times while over the water. Because I was missing longer than expected he came looking for me. When he saw where I was, he said , "What are you doing down there?" He pulled me out and the rest is history.

That's enough about me, this is **NOT** about **ME**, it's *ALL ABOUT HIM*!

Chapter 1
~ (Only The Father Knows) ~

The English Majority Text Version says it this way:
Mat 11:27 *All things have been delivered to Me by My Father, and <u>no one fully knows the Son except the Father</u>, nor does <u>anyone fully know</u> the Father except the Son, and* **"the one"** *to whom the* **Son wills to reveal** *Him.* **(EMTV)**

Jesus is saying that He certainly knows who the father is
and certainly the Father knows who the the Son is.
Jesus' **WORDS** are what is **RESPONSIBLE** for
all creation, He upholds ALL things by
The WORD of HIS Power ~ Heb 1:3.

The Easy To Read Version Says it this way:
Mat 11:27 - *"My Father has given me everything.* **No one** *knows the Son--<u>only the Father knows the Son</u>. And* **no one** *knows the Father--<u>only the Son knows the Father</u>. And the "<u>only people</u>" who will <u>know about the Father</u> are those the Son* **chooses** *to tell* **(ERV)**.

Jesus is The Creator,
He is The One that spoke in
Gen 1:1 ~~ Let There Be Light.
His WORDS was what was responsible
For the results.

Chapter 2
~~ It is imperative to KNOW "WHO" The Father is. ~~

Mat 24:32 *Learn a lesson from a fig tree. When its branches sprout and start putting out leaves, you know that summer is near.* ~~ **(Jesus is referring to Israel Becoming a Nation again)**

Mat 24:33 *So when you see all these things happening, you will know that the time has almost come.*
     ~~ **(Jesus is referring to being aware of The Signs of the Time)**

Mat 24:34 *I can promise you that some of the people of this generation will still be alive when all this happens.* ~~ **(Jesus is naming the TIME FRAME of His Return)**

Mat 24:35 *The sky and the earth won't last forever, but my words will.*

Mat 24:36 *No one knows the day or hour. The angels in heaven don't know, and the Son himself doesn't know. Only the Father knows.* **(CEV)**

Since "**ONLY**" The "**Father knows**" of The Return of Christ, that would be an Extremely important reason to know "**WHO THE FATHER**" IS!

Chapter 3
~~ The Prophetic Realm is About to Increase in 2015 ~~

~~ This next bit of information came from the "Elijah List." ~~

~~ Word Prophets by Dr. Theresa Phillips ~~

February 5, 2015 Get Ready!
Dr. Theresa Phillips

While in prayer over 2015, the Lord burst Himself into me. I could feel the presence so very strong. I began to travail over 2015, when the Lord began to speak to me. His first words were:

"NO FEAR, CHURCH. NO FEAR!"

At that moment, I began to sense more of the prophetic coming forth. Different spheres of prophecy for many different people. I wait ~~~

"The prophetic realm is about to increase! Some prophets will be emerging with a "FRESH revelation" which is in tune with Scripture that has been "dormant." Yes, (dormant), for I have "hidden" some of My Word for such a time as this," says the Lord.

"Oh yes, it's going to be an extremely insightful year packed with "*REVELATION*" ahead. *Pay attention to the prophets of the "WORD".* These prophetic utterances will adhere to the Holy Writ while they release "**REVELATION**" to My people. Many will become saved in the "**releasing of the Holy Writ.**"

This Book originates from "Heaven"! That's according to **John 3:27** - *John answered, "People can't receive anything unless it has been given to them from heaven.* **(GW)**

I am writing this book because Heaven spoke "**Six Little WORDS**" into my Spirit, that I heard audibly. This process started back in 1984.

Chapter 4
~~~ What was these ~ Six Little WORDS ~~~ ?

1) Nov 1, 1995 at 4:30 am, God spoke to me "In My Spirit"~~
~~ "*SPIRIT IS CONTAINER*" ~~

2) ~~ "**WORD IS FATHER** ~~ Nov. - 1996 @ 11:pm

~~ **Just before Jesus' Ascension** ~~

John 20:17 - *Jesus said to her, Do not put your hand on me, for I have not gone up to the Father: but go to "**my brothers**" and say to them, I go up to (**my Father**) and (**your Father**), to (**my God**) and (**your** God)* **(BBE).** ~~ **(Jesus is saying that He and YOU have THE SAME FATHER). (BBE)**

Well this is interesting! Jesus said that **YOUR** Father was **HIS** Father; and that **YOUR** God was **His** God. It should be evident that Jesus was telling the **Truth**, Right! Now what I am about to say is <u>not my words</u>; BUT words that I Heard ***FROM*** Heaven. November of 1996 @ 11:00 p.m., I heard these <u>three little WORDS</u>.

Chapter 5
~ ~ ~ ("**WORD IS FATHER**") ~ ~ ~

On November 1, of 1996; I was just falling asleep about 11:00 p.m., when at the foot of my bed I heard a very loud voice say these three words --- (**WORD IS FATHER**)! I asked my wife Sherri if she heard that, and she said, "I didn't hear anything!" These word were so loud to me that I had thought that I heard them with my outer ear; since then I have realized that God had spoken to my Spirit.

I immediately got out of bed and started writing. What I wrote down first was **1Pet 1:23** ~ *Being born again, not of corruptible seed, but of incorruptible, by the **word of God**, which liveth and abideth for ever* **(KJV).**

It says it this way in the **B**asic **B**ible **E**nglish - *Because you have had a new birth, <u>not from</u> <u>the **seed** of man</u>, but from **eternal seed**, <u>through the **"word"**</u> of a living and unchanging God.*

Most people understand that Jesus was born the Son of God, but not realizing that Jesus is also the **Father** <u>with flesh</u> on.

Joh 14:8 *Philip told him, "Lord, show us the Father, and that will satisfy us." {9} "Have I been with you all this time, Philip, and you still do not know me?" Jesus asked him. "The person who has seen **me** has seen **the Father**. So how can you say, 'Show us **the Father**'? {10} You believe, don't you, that I am in **the Father** and **the Father** is in* <u>me</u>? *The words that I say to you I do not speak on my own.* (The **Child**) *It is the Father* ~ (**The Spirit of God**) ~ *who dwells in me and who carries out his work.* (Through My **WORDS**) **(ISV).**

Jesus just told Philip that "<u>HE</u>" was THE "FATHER".
Jesus was the temporal manifestation of THE WORD ~
Jn 1:14 ~ and the WORD was made flesh and dwelt among us.
Jesus' WORDS give Fatherhood to creation ~ Jesus' WORDS
Became Flesh ~ Jesus as <u>Son of God</u>. Inside Jesus' Temporal body

Was His SPIRIT ~ which is HOLY and Eternal.

Deu 6:4 Hear, O Israel: The LORD our God *is* one LORD: (KJV)

Heb 1:3 *Who being the brightness of his glory, and the <u>express image</u> of his person, and upholding all things by the "**<u>word of his power</u>**", when he had by himself purged <u>our sins</u>, sat down on the right hand of the Majesty on high;* **(KJV)**

God runs His Kingdom **<u>with</u>** and **<u>by</u>** His "**<u>WORD</u>**."

Chapter 6
~~~ Who was in The Beginning? ~~~

Joh 1:1 *In the beginning was the <u>**Word**</u>, and the <u>**Word**</u> was with God, and the <u>**Word**</u> was God.*
~~~ **(Jesus is The Creator of ALL things, it was Jesus who was Speaking all the WORDS).**

Joh 1:2 *He was in the beginning <u>**with God**</u>.* **(These WORDS were with Jesus to be Spoken).**

Joh 1:3 *All things came into being <u>**through Him**</u>, and <u>**without Him**</u> not even one thing came into being that has come into being.* **(LEB)** ~~~ **(Again Jesus is The Creator and HE did it ALL With WORDS).**

Joh 1:4 *In <u>**Him**</u> was life, and the life was the light of men;* **(LEB)** ~~~ **(In Jesus was The Holy Spirit and His Plan was to Bring That Spirit OF LIFE to ALL Who would Receive HIM)**

Joh 1:5 *and the light shines in the darkness, and the darkness did not overtake it.* **(LEB)** ~~~ **(Jesus was The Only One on Planet Earth that had The Holy Spirit, and No One could do away with it).**

Joh 1:6 *There was a man sent from God; his name was John.* **(LEB)** ~~~ **(Jesus will do nothing without telling His Servants the Prophets FIRST ~ Amos 3:7**

Joh 1:7 *He came for a witness, that he might witness concerning the Light, that all might believe through Him.* **(LEB)**

Joh 1:8 *He was not that Light, but that he might witness concerning the Light.*
Joh 1:9 *He was the true Light; He **enlightens every man coming into the world**.* **(Jesus is The One that Turns Your Spirit From Darkness to LIGHT). ~ Col 1:13**
.
Joh 1:10 *He was in the world, and the world came into being through Him, yet the world did not know Him.* **(LEB) ~~ (Jesus had created the Earth that they were all standing on, and because all that were there with Him, had the king of darkness for their FATHER ~ no one had a clue who Jesus was. ~ Joh 8:44.**

Joh 1:11 *He came to **His own**,* ~~~ **(((" ALL of Satan's Kids")))** ~~~ *and **His own** did not receive Him.* **(LEB) ~~ (There was no one there that Jesus hadn't CREATED ~~ yet BECAUSE of their Spiritual Father, They Lived In Darkness).**

Joh 1:12 *But as many as received Him, to them He gave authority to become **children of God**, to the ones believing into His name,* **(LEB) ~~ (For ALL that Received Him, Received His Spirit AGAIN ~ Tit 3:5)**

Joh 1:13 *who were born **not of blood**, nor of the **will of the flesh**, nor of **the will of man**, but were **born of God**.* **(LEB) ~~ (1Pe 1:3 *Blessed be the God and Father of our Lord Jesus Christ, He according to His great mercy having <u>REgenerated</u> us to a living hope through the resurrection of Jesus Christ from the dead,* (MKJV)**

1Pe 1:4 *to an inheritance incorruptible and undefiled and unfading, having been kept in Heaven for you* **{5}** *the ones in the power of God being guarded through faith to a salvation <u>ready to be revealed in the last time</u>;)* **(LITV)**

Joh 1:14 *And the ("**<u>Word</u>**") became (""**<u>flesh</u>**") and tabernacled among us. And we beheld His glory, glory as of an only begotten from the Father, full of grace and of truth.* **(LITV) ~~ (Jesus became the fulfillment of Isa 9:6)**

Joh 1:15 *John witnesses concerning Him, and has cried out, saying, This One was He of whom I said, He coming after me has been before me, for He was preceding me.* **(John was Jesus' chosen one to Speak Into Existence the REALITY of Who Jesus was). (LITV)**

Joh 1:16 *And out of His fullness we all received, and **"grace on top of grace"**. (LITV) ~~~*
(Eph 2:7-10; Rom 5:9; Rom 10:9&10; Rom 10?:13; Col1 :18; Eph 2:5; Eph 2:8; Tit 3:5).

Joh 1:17 *For the Law was given through Moses, but **grace and truth** came through **Jesus Christ**. (LITV)*

Chapter 7
~~~ Inserting *WHO* The <u>WORD</u> was ~~~

Joh 1:1 *In the beginning the **<u>Word</u>** ~ **"(JESUS)"** ~ already existed. The **<u>Word</u>** ~ **"(JESUS)"**~ was with God ~ **"(JESUS)"** ~, and the **<u>Word</u>** ~ **"(JESUS)"** ~ was God* **(<u>JESUS</u>).** ~

Joh 1:2 *<u>He</u> ~ **"(JESUS)"**~ was already with <u>God</u> ~ **"(JESUS)"** ~ in the beginning.* ~

Joh 1:3 *Everything came into existence through him ~ **"(JESUS)."** ~ Not one thing that exists was made without <u>him</u> ~ **"(JESUS)".**~*

Joh 1:4 *He ~ **"(JESUS)"** ~ was the source of life, and that life was the light for humanity.*

Joh 1:5 *The light shines in the dark, and the dark has never extinguished it.*

Joh 1:6 *God sent a man named John to be his messenger.*

Joh 1:7 *John came to declare the truth about the light so that everyone would become believers through **<u>his</u>** message. ~ (**THE WORD**)*
Joh 1:8 *John was not the light, but he came to declare the truth about the light.*

Joh 1:9 *The real light, which shines on everyone, was coming into the world.*

Joh 1:10 *<u>He</u> ~ **"(JESUS)"** ~ was in the world, and the world came into existence through <u>him</u> ~**"(JESUS)."** ~ Yet, the world didn't recognize <u>him</u> ~ **"(JESUS)".** ~*
Joh 1:11 *<u>He</u> ~ **"(JESUS)"** ~ went to <u>his</u> own people, and <u>his</u> own people didn't accept him.* ~~~

~ (Jesus) ~

Joh 1:12 *However, **<u>he</u>** ~ **"(JESUS)"** ~ gave the right to become God's children to everyone who believed in <u>him</u> ~ **"(JESUS)."** ~*

Joh 1:13 *These people didn't become* <u>God's</u> ~ **(Jesus')** ~ *children in a physical way-from a human impulse or from a husband's desire to have a child. They were born from* <u>God</u> ~ **"(JESUS)."**

Joh 1:14 *The* <u>Word</u> ~ **"(JESUS)"** ~ *became human and lived among us. We saw* <u>his</u> ~ **"(JESUS)"**~ *glory. It was the glory that the* **Father** ~ **"(JESUS)"** ~ *shares with his only* <u>Son</u> ~ **"(JESUS),"** ~ *a glory full of kindness and truth.*

Joh 1:15 *John declared the truth about* <u>him</u> ~ **"(*JESUS*)"** ~ *when he said loudly, "This is the* <u>person</u> ~ **"(JESUS)"** ~ *about whom I said, 'The* <u>one</u> ~ **"(JESUS)"** ~ *who comes after me was before me because* <u>he</u> ~ **"(JESUS)"** ~ *existed before I did.'")*

Joh 1:16 *Each of us has received one gift after another because of all that the* <u>Word</u> ~ **"(JESUS)"**~ *is.*

Joh 1:17 *The Teachings were given through Moses, but* <u>kindness and truth</u> *came into existence through **Jesus Christ**.* ~ **(KJV)**

~~~~~~

Isa 28:10 *For* <u>precept</u> *must be upon* <u>precept</u>, <u>precept</u> *upon* <u>precept</u>; <u>line</u> *upon* <u>line</u>, <u>line</u> *upon* <u>line</u>;
here a <u>little</u>, *and there a* <u>little:</u> **(KJV)** ~~~

The Bible is like a puzzle ~ If your ~ <u>precepts</u> ~ are wrong then your ~ **CONCEPTS** ~ are wrong also. The more pieces of a puzzle you put together, the better chance to understand the **BIGGER** picture.

The bible is like a puzzle, Jesus said that after we have been born from Heaven, we should desire the sincere Milk of the Word that we should grow thereby. Milk is an easier substance for a baby to digest; a baby has no teeth to chew meat with. If we are not getting the milk of the Word then there is no way for us to grow Spiritually. The bible teaches that there should come a time in our development ~ spiritually ~ that we all should be teachers of the Word; but the reference is that you need to be taught again the first principles of God's Kingdom all over again.

The people that can chew and digest the strong Meat of the Word, are the fully mature, discerning both Good and Evil. **(Heb 5:12-14)**

Hopefully we have now established that :

    1) The Father is The **Word.**

    2) Jesus is The ("**Father")** with ("**flesh")** on.

    3) Jesus is The one Speaking God's **Word.**

    4) The **WORDS** that Jesus speaks Creates Everything.

    5) Adam was Jesus' Brother ~ Both were **Son's of God**.

        6) Mat 20:*16 So the **last** shall be **first**, and the **first** **last**. **(ASV)**

7) God shows us the End From the Beginning. In as much as **Adam was God with flesh on** and we are ~ "**Now as He is**". **1Jn 4:17** *Herein is our love made perfect, that we may have boldness in the day of judgment: because **as he is**, so "**are we"** in this world.* **(KJV)**

The majority of the time when Jesus is speaking, He's speaking Spiritually and the natural man cannot understand Him.

1Co 2:9 *But as Scripture says: "No eye has seen, no ear has heard, and no mind has imagined the things that God has prepared for those who love him." {10} God has **revealed those things to us by his Spirit**. The Spirit searches everything, **especially the deep things of God**. {11} After all, who knows everything about a person except that person's own spirit? In the same way**, no one** has **known everything about God** except **God's Spirit**.* **(GW)**

Chapter 8
~~~ Where did all this begin? ~~~

The process that was taken to accumulate this information, took place over a 32 year period of time. I really got involved with this project when the Holy Spirit asked me one question!

  He asked me how I could be (**"*in Christ")*** and be (**"*DEAD")***?

That would be in reference to **(KJV) 1Th 4:16** *For the Lord himself shall descend from heaven with a shout, with the voice of the archangel, and with the trump of God: and the **dead in Christ** shall rise first:*

So this journey the Lord had me on began; first to let Him teach me what **He** Meant by **DEAD** and what He Meant by **LIFE**. **(DEAD means to be SEPARATED from The LIFE of God; and LIFE means to be in The Presence of GOD.**

~~~ The most difficult lesson that The Holy Spirit taught me was this: ~~~

One Wednesday evening service at the Dresden Community Church I was teaching **on Daniel 9:24-27** and while speaking ~~~ I started hearing The Holy Spirit telling me what to say ~~~ **I was so excited I could hardly contain myself.** When it can time for me to quit speaking ~ HE Told me When I was DONE. So I went and sat down on the third row back from the front, the Isle seat; I sat there about 10 seconds, and The Lord spoke to me and said, **THEY NEVER HEARD A WORD YOU SAID!!!**

I SAID YOU'RE KIDDING ME!!! ~~~ For the next two weeks I was completely beside myself. I didn't read my bible, I didn't really want to go to church, I was in *TOTAL CONFUSION* to say the least! I said God I don't understand, ~ YOU Told Me What To Say, then YOU Tell Me that They Never Heard A Word I Said..... I know that The Bible states that "God is not The Author of Confusion **BUT** ~~~ when God says anything He is NEVER Confused about it.

He wasn't confused, ***BUT*** I was; then He asked me a question. Have you been taught that You can get Ahead of Me? I said yes, and do you think that it is possible that you can do things on your own and Get Ahead of Me? I said NO LORD ~~~ I at least KNOW better than That. He said I want you to know that I am in Complete Control of My Kingdom, and no one will ever get ahead of Me.

He said that His Anointing was not only for me to speak His Word; But that it also took His Anointing of the peoples ears ~~~ to **HEAR WHAT** was being said. In reality I have been practicing speaking His Word on **Daniel 9:24-27** and about the things in this book ~~~ fully knowing that His words that He gave me was **still** falling on **Deaf Ears**. ~~~ (I believe **THAT** is about to **CHANGE**.)

So NOTHING on Planet Earth, for any of His events, will happen ,WITHOUT Him leading the whole thing. Let's just say that He is in Charge of ALL things; And I am SOOO Grateful that HE IS!
Now the best part is when **FAITH** *Graduates* it turns into ~~~ **TRUST.** ~ **(I TRUST YOU LORD).**

~~~~~~

(KJV) **John 1:1** *In the **beginning** was the **Word**, and the **Word** was **with God**, and the **Word was God**.* - Well I *think* that is pretty clear, don't you! **Everything** in existence today and what ever there **will be, originates** with the **WORDS** that God **Speaks**! Jesus is **the one** that **Speaks** these words --- (**WORD IS FATHER**); Jesus said in **John 14:9** *Anyone who has **seen me** has **seen the Father**! So **why** are you asking to see him?* **(TLB)**

Jesus is "**The Father**", He is the **One Speaking** ALL these **CREATIVE WORDS** that are referred to in **Colossians 1:16** *Christ himself is the Creator who made everything in heaven and earth, the things we can see and the things we can't; the spirit world with its kings and kingdoms, its rulers and authorities; all were made by Christ for his own use and glory* **(TLB)**. God's word is quite special ~~~ There would be nothing without His **Words** ~ ever!!!

Jesus said in ~~~ **John 6:63** *Only the Holy Spirit gives eternal life. Those born only once, with physical birth, will never receive this gift. But now I have told you how to get this true spiritual life.*

Joh 3:3 *Jesus replied, "I tell you for certain that you must be **born from above** before you can see God's kingdom!"* **(CEV)**

Jesus' words are Spirit and Life; Without His Words
there would be **no spirit** and **no life**.

Chapter 9
~~~ Jesus' Credentials from The Old Testament ~~~

Let's now look into The Old Testament to SEE ~ "(**JESUS'**)" ~ credentials.

Isa 9:6 *For unto us a **child** is born, ~ (**Jesus**)unto us a **son** ~ (**Jesus**) ~ is given: and the government shall be upon his ~ (**Jesus**) ~ shoulder: and his name ~ (**Jesus**) ~ shall be called **Wonderful, Counsellor**, **The mighty "God"**, **The everlasting "Father"**, **The Prince of Peace*** (KJV).

The **Son** ~ (**Jesus**) ~ is called Wonderful, and indeed He is Wonderful!
 (Do you remember what it was like to be in this world without Him?)

The **Son** ~ (**Jesus**) ~ is called counselor,
As Counselor where would we all be without his "**WORD**" to lead and guide our lives?

The **Son** ~ (Jesus) ~ is called ~~~ "**THE MIGHTY "GOD**",
Of which He is, He is "THE **WORD**" made flesh and in the beginning was "The **WORD**".

This **Son** ~ (Jesus) ~ is called, "**THE EVERLASTING "FATHER"**!

So The Bible (which is God's "**WORD**", says that JESUS is ~ The **Father.** The Holy Spirit said to me that - ~ **(WORD IS FATHER)** ~. In the beginning was The **~ WORD ~,** The **WORD** was with GOD and THE ~ **WORD** ~ was God. Who was Speaking the **WORDS** of God, none other than ~ **JESUS** ~. **Deu 6:4** *Hear, O Israel: The LORD our God is **one** LORD*: **(KJV)**

In **Isaiah 9:6** it state that this child ~ Jesus is; "The Wonderful **Counselor**", ~ "The Mighty **God**", ~ "The Everlasting **Father**", ~ "The **Prince of Peace**."

        This child that was born, was the **FATHER** with flesh on.
This Child that could be seen was **Temporal**, But His "**SPIRIT**" came from God, which is **Eternal**, and could **NOT** be seen.

2Co 4:18 *because we are not looking at what is seen, but what **is not seen**. For what is seen is temporary, but what is **not seen** is **eternal*** **(LEB).**

John 6:63 *It is the spirit that quickeneth; the flesh profiteth nothing: the **words** that I speak unto you, they are **spirit**, and they are **life**.* **(KJV)**

Jesus said in **Mat 11:27** *My Father has given me everything, and he is **the only one** who knows the Son. The **only one** who truly knows the Father is the Son. But the **Son wants to tell others** about **the Father**, so that they can **know** him too.* **(CEV)**

 Mat 24:3 *As Jesus sat on the Mount of Olives, the disciples came to him in private. "Tell us when all this will be," they asked, "and what will happen to show that it is the time for your coming and the end of the age."* **(GNB)**

Mat 24:36 *"**No one** knows, however, when that day and hour will come ~~~ **neither the angels** in heaven **nor the Son**; the (((**"Father alone")))** knows.* **(GNB)**

Chapter 10
~~~ Who is This Child? ~~~

Isaiah 9:6 *For unto us a **Child is Born**, unto us s **Son is given**: and the government shall be upon his shoulder: and his name shall be called **Wonderful, Counslor**, The **Mighty God**, The **Everlasting Father**, The **Prince of Peace**. {7} Of the increase of his **government** and peace there shall be no end, upon the throne of David, and upon his kingdom, to order it, and to establish it with judgment and with justice from henceforth even for ever. The zeal of the LORD of hosts will perform this.* **(KJV)**

> **1)** The Kingdom of God is <u>not</u> a **Religion**!
> **2)** Jesus is not a **President!**
> **3)** Jesus is a **King!**
> **4)** His Kingdom is a **Government**!

This **child** was born, but **The Son** never was!

A) Why was the Son never born?

1) The **Son** is Jesus and is Eternal,
> The **Son** is Jesus ~ The One Called Wonderful.
> The **Son** is Jesus ~ The Counselor,
> The **Son** is Jesus ~ The Mighty God.
> The **Son** is Jesus ~ The Everlasting Father,
> The **Son** is Jesus ~ The Prince of Peace.

2) The Child that was born was **Temporal** and was only **flesh.**
> **1 Cor 15:50** Now this I say, brethren, that **flesh** and
> **Blood cannot** inherit the Kingdom of God. **(KJV)**

3) Jesus said in **John 3:6** *That which is born of the **flesh is flesh**; and that which is born of the **Spirit is Spirit**.* **Jn 4:24** *God is a **Spirit.*** **(KJV)**

A) In order to walk around on planet earth you need an <u>earth suit</u> called <u>the flesh.</u>

B) Jas 2:26 *For as the body **without a spirit** is dead, so also faith without works is dead.* **(DARBY)**

> **C)** We are Spirit Beings, that live in an earth suit; the spirit is called ,
> "The **Inner Man**,"and our **Soul Lives** inside the "**INNER MAN**."
> **1 Cor 15:44** says, There is a **Natural** body, and there is a **Spiritual** body.

4) John 3:5 says, *Jesus answered, Verily, verily, I say unto thee, Except a man be born of **water and** of the **Spirit**, he cannot enter into the   kingdom of God.* **(KJV)** ~~~ (water means water of the womb)

5) We all were in His Kingdom before we were born on planet earth, this is the only reason the Son was given unto us; was to redeem us. (redeem means to **buy back**) ~~~

1 Cor 6:19 says, *What? know ye not that your body is the temple of the Holy Ghost which is in you, which ye have of God, and ye are not your own? {20} For ye are **bought with a price**: therefore glorify God in your body, and in **your spirit, which are God's**.* **(KJV)**

Jesus' **Temporary Body** was born through the **Water of the Womb** but His spirit came from, "**The Father**". ~ (Through His **WORD** in **Isa 9:6**) So the physical, temporary, body (or earth suit) of Jesus came through Mary ~ Which made Him **The Son of Man**.

6) (KJV) 2 Cor 4:18 says, *While we look not at the things which are seen, but at the things which are not seen: for the things which **are seen are temporal**; but the things which are **not seen are eternal.*** **(KJV)**

-
The **Child** that was born was **temporal**, but **The Son** that was given was **Eternal.**
The Child that was born could be seen, and therefore was temporal, The Son was **THE INNER MAN** of Jesus, which was the **Spiritual Body** and could **not be seen** and therefore eternal.

> And the spirit that gave Him **Life** came from His **Father.**
> **A)** And who is His Father?
>> **1)** His Father is the **WORD**!
>> **2)** The **WORD** is your Father also .

(KJV) John 20:17 Jesus said, Touch me not; for I am not yet ascended to my Father: but go to my brethren, and say unto them, I ascend unto my Father, **and your Father**; and *to **my God, and your God***. ~

Chapter 11
~~~ (**WORD** *IS* **FATHER.)** ~~~

Well let's look at the definition of the word Father:

(From Easton's Bible Dict.)
>   **(1.)** A name applied to any ancestor
>   **(2.)** As a **title** of respect to a chief, ruler, or elder, etc.
>   **(3.)** The author or **beginner of anything** is also so called Father
>   **(4.)** Applied to God **(Jesus)**

Webster's Dictionary:
>   **a)** The male parent or **ancestor.**
>   **b)** An **originator**
>   **c)** The **OLDEST** member of a community.
>   **d)** To be the **FATHER** of.
>   **e)** To fix the **ORIGINAL** responsibility for.

It helps to understand that **Father** is a position, a **place of authority**, one who is **RESPONSIBLE** for: Who was Responsible for **CREATING EVERYTHING**, **JESUS** was!!! Jesus' **WORDS** are the "**FATHER**" or the means by which **ALL** things were brought into existence!

God runs His kingdom with "**HIS WORDS**". That's the ONLY way you got born **FROM ABOVE**, (**again**). This is the **only way** you can get into God's Kingdom ~~~

1 Peter 1:23 *Being **born again**, not of corruptible seed, but of **incorruptible**, **by the word of God**, which liveth and abideth for ever.* **(KJV)** ~~~ Now you can better understand ~~~

John 1:12 *But as many as **received him**, to them gave he **power to become** the sons of God, even to them that believe on his name*: **(KJV)**

It takes God's **POWER** to **destroy the body of sin** and to give you **HIS SPIRITUAL BODY**. We **ARE** the **BODY** of Christ and He is THE "**HEAD**". The Resurrection has made **US** all **ONE.**

In summary: Jesus is The Creator; He created everything by speaking "**WORDS**". The "**WORDS**" that He **Spoke** is the **originator** of everything that came into being. No words nothing happens. Jesus is the author of the Bible; He is also the Author of **Isaiah 9:6** which He states that a **child** would be born; His title will be "The Mighty **God**" ~~~ "The Everlasting **FATHER**"! Jesus spoke those word **732** years before **He became** what He **spoke!** And "**THE WORD**" was made flesh, and dwelt among us, (**word is Father**)!!!

Jesus said in ~~ **John 10:30** _I and **my Father** are **one**_ **(KJV).** In **John 14:9** Jesus said, _"He that hath seen **ME** hath seen **THE FATHER**"_**(BBE).** "**THE WORD IS FATHER**". Jesus is God ~ the words that he speaks have the power in them to do whatever He commands!

Chapter 12
~~~ The Son is also Jehovah ~~~

1) Prov 16:4 says - **_Jehovah_** _hath made everything for it's own end; Yea, underline even the wicked for the day of evil_ **(ASV)**.

2) Isa 40:28 says, _Hast thou not known? Hast thou not heard? The everlasting God._ **_"Jehovah the Creator"_** _of the ends of the earth, fainteth not, neither is weary;there is no searching of his understanding_ **(KJV)**.

3) Jer 10:10 _But **Jehovah** is the true **God**; he is the living God, and an **everlasting King**: at his wrath the earth trembleth, and the nations are not able to abide his indignation._ **(ASV)**

4) And who is **Jehovah**? Jehovah is **JESUS ~ "CREATOR"**

Chapter 13
~~~ What is Life? ~~~

JESUS PRESENTS
John 14:20

("*At That Day*") --- ye shall know that I am *in my Father*, and *you in me*, and *I in you*.

Mat. 11:27 Jesus said, All things have been delivered to Me by My Father, and *no one* knows the *Son* except the *Father*. Nor does *anyone* know the Father *except the Son*, and the one to whom *the Son* wills to *reveal* Him.

God has made us a three part being --- *Body – Soul & Spirit*
The BODY has <u>TWO parts</u> – There is a *NATURAL* body & There is a *SPIRITUAL body* – The *NATURAL* body cannot move without a *SPIRITUAL* body in it!

James 2:26 For as the body *without the spirit* is dead, so faith without works is dead also.

By Ron Dyer
March 1. 2010

1Jn 5:12 *He that **hath the Son** hath life; and he that **hath not the Son** of God **hath not** life.*

~~~ **Through GRACE** ~~~

From The **Second** ADAM:
  1. Father is now **God.**   **(John 20:17)**

2. Peace with God.   **(Rom. 5:1)**
3. Saints.   **(1 Cor, 1:2)**
4. Walk in The **Spirit**.   **(Gal 5:16)**
5. 1 lave put on the **NEW** man.   **(Eph. 4:24)**
6. Body of Sin Destroyed   **(Rom. 6:6)**
7. Passed **From** DEATH to <u>**Life**</u>.   **(John 5:24)**
8. <u>**Alive**</u> From the **DEAD**   **(Rom 6:13)**
9. By MAN came The <u>**Resurrection**</u>"! **(1 Cor. 15:21)**
10. <u>WE ARE NOW</u> AS **"HE IS".**   **(IJohn4:17)** ~~~
Now we are back in Heaven: Born FROM There **John 3:3** ~~~ **Eph 2:6** *So that we came back from death with him, and <u>are seated with him in the heavens</u>, in Christ Jesus;* **(BBE)**

       John 5:40 *And ye will not come to me, that ye might have <u>**life**</u>.* **(KJV)** ~~ **John 5:40** *Yet you won't come to me so that <u>**I can give**</u> you this <u>**life eternal!**</u>* **(TLB)** ~~ Have you ever noticed that when Jesus is speaking, He talks more about <u>**eternal**</u> things than temporary. That's what He came to do; He came to make an Eternal "<u>**separation**</u>" of the <u>**two**</u> kingdoms.

Life is what Adam was given when God gave him His <u>spiritual</u> body, that's what **LIFE IS**, having your <u>**SOUL**</u> inside God's **spiritual body;** ~~~ Likewise DEATH is having your <u>**SOUL**</u> inside Satan's Spiritual Body! Jesus said He wanted to give you this spiritual body, that makes it quite clear that it is something we weren't born with ~~~ **John 3:6** *That which is <u>**born of the flesh**</u> is flesh; and that which is <u>**born of the Spirit**</u> is spirit. {7} Marvel not that I said unto thee, ye must be <u>**born from above**</u>.* -**(KJV)** ~~~

1 Corinthians 15:48 *Every human being has a body just <u>**like Adam's,**</u> made of dust, but all who <u>**become**</u> Christ's will have the <u>**same kind of body as his**</u> ~~~ a body <u>**from heaven**</u>.* **(TLB)**

1 Corinthians 15:50 *I tell you this, my brothers: an <u>**earthly body**</u> made of <u>flesh</u> and blood <u>**cannot**</u> get <u>**into God's**</u> Kingdom. These perishable bodies of ours <u>**are not**</u> the right <u>**kind**</u> to live <u>**forever**</u>.* **(TLB)**

       First off Christ is not Jesus' last name; the word **Christ** simply means "**Anointed**". It's Jesus, **The Anointed**! In **Gen. 3:15** the promise of The "Redeemer" is made. From Adam to the cross they were looking for a Redeemer, for all that obeyed God's word. They were **in Christ** as much as we are; the difference being they had received **the promise** of salvation that Jesus had **not yet paid** for! They were still in the same spiritual body they were born in, **(corruptible** from their **father)** ~~ earthly and spiritual. ~

Chapter 14
~~~ What is DEATH? ~~~
Definition of DEATH = Separation <u>FROM</u> ~~~ the <u>LIFE</u> of God.

This is how Adam <u>**DIED**</u>, The <u>**SAME**</u> Day he <u>**Disobeyed**</u> Jesus.

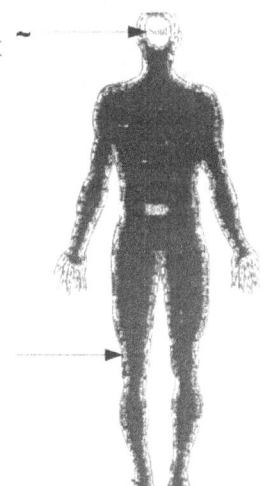

Gen 2:16 *But the LORD told him, "You may eat fruit from any tree in the garden.*
Gen 2:17 *<u>except</u> the one that **has the power** to let you know the <u>**difference**</u> between <u>**right and wrong**</u>. If you eat any fruit from that tree, you will die <u>**before the day is over!**</u>" (CEV)*

Adam's SOUL ~ <u>**ETERNAL**</u>
Now <u>**INSIDE**</u> Satan's <u>**BODY**</u>

It is quite evident that Jesus was not talking about PHYSICAL DEATH ~~~ Jesus was talking about SPIRITUAL DEATH ~~~ Which is Separation from the life of God.

Gen 5:5 *And all the days that Adam lived were nine hundred and thirty years: and he died.* (KJV) ~~~ This was his <u>PHYSICAL DEATH.</u>

Adam's Physical Body can be seen and only Temporal.

It only took <u>11 One Hundredths</u> of a <u>**SECOND**</u> for ADAM to change FATHERS ~~~ Adam was changed from Jesus' Kingdom of <u>**LIGHT**</u> ~~~ To Satan's kingdom of <u>**DARKNESS**</u> ~ <u>**IN THE TWINKLING OF AN EYE.**</u>

This is how Jesus DIED ~~~ SEPARATED from His Father.

Adam fell from "THE GLORY"
through <u>DISOBEDIENCE</u> and JESUS Yielded up "THE <u>GLORY</u>" back to the FATHER and
became SIN for US ~ Just like we were!!!

2Co 5:21 *For he hath made him to be sin for us, who knew no sin; that we might be made the righteousness of God in him.* **(KJV)**

Jas 2:26 *For as the body without a spirit is dead, so also faith without works is dead.* **(DARBY)**

The only way a person can be alive physically on planet Earth is to have a Spirit being "inside their physical body". There is only two choices for what Spirit that will be. When you are born from your mothers womb, you received the spirit that came through your <u>**Earthly father**</u> ~ which is <u>**Satan's Spirit**</u>. In order to go to Heaven, you have to have God's Spirit.

In order to receive God's Spirit; You have to be born AGAIN or ANEW. Jesus describes it this way. **John 3:6** *That which is **born of the flesh** is flesh; and that which is **born of the Spirit** is spirit. {7} Marvel not that I said unto thee, ye must be **born from above**.* **(KJV)**

1 John 5:12 *He that hath the Son **hath life**; and he that **hath not the Son** of God **hath not life**.* **(KJV)**

IN CHRIST

Jesus wants you to know and understand how these truths apply to your spiritual understanding of how you got -

"IN CHRIST"

Eph. 3:3 Paul says, - How that by *revelation* he made known unto me *the mystery, which is:*

That he might gather together *in one* all things *in Christ*, both which are in heaven, and which are on earth;

The WORD of The Lord came to me on Nov. 1. 1995 @ 4:30 A.M. And this is is what I heard!

"SPIRIT IS CONTAINER"

The Spiritual Body is the Container for our Soul

Your "Spirit" is The Container for Your "SOUL" and can be Separated by GOD'S "WORD"

Heb 4:12 *For God's Message is full of life and power, and is keener than the sharpest two-edged sword. It pierces even to the severance of soul from spirit, and penetrates between the joints and the marrow, and it can discern the secret thoughts and purposes of the heart. (WNT)*

(Adam's body of Dirt)   "Temporal"

Gen 2:7 *And the LORD God formed man of the dust of the ground*

and breathed into his nostrils the breath of life;
Holy Spirit --- "Dotted Line "Eternal"

and man became a living soul.
"Eternal"

"Adam was "GOD" IN THE "FLESH"

Rom 3:23 *All of us have sinned and "fallen" short of "God's glory. " (KJV)*

Gen 2:16 *But the LORD told him, "You may eat fruit from any tree in the garden,*

Gen 2:17 *except the one that has the power to let you know the difference between right and wrong. If you eat any fruit from that tree, you will die before the day is over!" (CEV)*

Gen 5:5 *And all the days that Adam lived were nine hundred and thirty years: and he died. (KJV)*

Well that shouldn't be too difficult to understand. If you have received Jesus as your Savior, you received his **resurrected spiritual body**; which is **LIFE.**

Col 2:11 *In whom also ye __are circumcised__ with the circumcision __made without hands__, in __putting off__ the __body of the sins__ of the flesh __by__ the __circumcision of Christ__*: **(KJV)** If the **spirit of God** hasn't **made** you into a **NEW CREATION**, you are **DEAD**!

Why do you say, I'm dead? I didn't **GOD DID**. Jesus said in **John 14:6** *I am __the way__, __the truth__, and __the life__: no man cometh unto the Father, but __by me__.* **(KJV)**

Jesus also said in **(TLB) John 11:25** *"__I am__ the one __who raises the dead__ and gives them __life again__". Anyone who believes in me, __even though he dies__ like anyone else, shall __live again__.* **(TLB)**

There are only **two kingdoms,** God's Kingdom and Satan's. God's kingdom is, "The Kingdom of **Light**" and Satan's is, the kingdom of **darkness.** Let's compare the two kingdoms:

The kingdom of **DARKNESS** ~~~ **Jud 1:6** *And __the angels which kept not their first estate__, but left their own habitation, he hath reserved in everlasting chains __under darkness__ unto the judgment of the great day.* **(KJV)**

This spiritual body, that had been separated, from God's Spiritual body, is a **body of death**, (body of **sin**). **Rom 5:12** *Wherefore, as by one man __sin entered into the world__, and __death by sin__; and so __death__ passed __upon all men__, for that __all have sinned__:* **(KJV)** ~~~

SIN is not just what you do against **GOD"S WORD** ~~~ It is **THE WAY YOU WERE BORN on Planet Earth;** unless you get born again (***FROM*** ABOVE) you will be ***ETERNALY SEPARATED*** from God's Kingdom. Forever and Ever and Ever!!!

Rom 3:*23* *All of us have sinned and fallen short of God's glory.* **(CEV)** ~~~ **We** all **had** the **glory** but; "The wages of Sin is **Death**. That means **SEPARATED** from the **LIFE OF GOD**!

From The **First** ADAM:
1. Ye are of your father the **devil**   (John 8:44)
2. Enemies of God   (Rom. 5:10)
3. Ungodly   (Rom. 5:6)

4. Everyone **Disobedient**   (Rom. 5:19)
5. Old Man Eph. 4:22, Col. 3:9   (Rom. 6:6)
6. Body of **Sin**   (Rom. 6:6)
7. Body of **Death**   (Rom. 7:24)
8. Ye who were **Dead**   (Eph.2; I)
9. Everyone Born **Dead**   (Rom. 5:12)
10. By man came **DEATH**   (1 Cor. 15:21)

1 Corinthians 15:22 *Everyone dies because* <u>*all of us*</u> *are related to Adam, being members of his sinful race, and wherever there* <u>*is sin, death results.*</u> *But all who are related to Christ will rise again.* **(TLB)**.

Col 3:1 *Since you were brought back to life with Christ, focus on the things that are above ~* **(GW)**

Again, Adam had been given God's Spirit of <u>LIFE</u> in creation, and Adam lost God's Spirit through <u>disobedience</u> and the above list applies to everyone born on planet earth, with Jesus being the only exception! Jesus' Father was. **"THE "WORD" OF GOD"**

Chapter 15
~~~ How Jesus Died ~~~

Heb 4:12 *For the* <u>*word of God*</u> *is living and full of power, and is sharper than any two-edged sword, cutting through and* ***making a division*** *even of (((("***the soul and the spirit"***))), the bones and the muscles, and quick to see the thoughts and purposes of the heart.* **(BBE)**

That is exactly what happened to Adam; when he disobeyed Jesus in the garden, Jesus **SERPRATED** his **SOUL** from His **SPIRIT**.

Gen 2:17 *But of the fruit of the tree of the knowledge of good and evil you may not take; for* ***on the day*** *when you take of it,* ***death will certainly come to you.*** **(BBE)** ~~

That **Day** Adam **DIED** in the **twinkling of an eye** Jesus withdrew **HIS SPIRIT** and put **Adam's SOUL** in **Satan's Spirit**.

This was THE way Jesus could DIE

1Co 2:1 *Brothers and sisters, when I came to you, I didn't speak about God's **mystery** as if it were some kind of brilliant message or wisdom.*
1Co 2:2 *While I was with you, I decided to deal with only one subject ~ Jesus Christ, who was crucified.*

1Co 2:3 *When I came to you, I was weak. I was afraid and very nervous.*
1Co 2:4 *I didn't speak my message with persuasive intellectual arguments. I spoke my message with a show of spiritual power*

1Co 2:5 *so that **your faith would not be based on human wisdom but on God's power**.*
1Co 2:6 *However, we do use **wisdom to speak to those who are "mature"**. It is a wisdom that doesn't belong to this world or to the rulers of this world **who are in power today** and gone tomorrow.*

1Co 2:7 *We speak about **the mystery of God's wisdom**. It is a wisdom that has been hidden, which God had planned **for our glory** before the world began.*
1Co 2:8 *Not one of the **rulers of this world has known** it. If they had, they **wouldn't have crucified the Lord of glory**.*

1Co 2:9 *But as Scripture says: "No eye has seen, no ear has heard, and no mind has imagined the things that God has prepared for those who love him."*
1Co 2:10 ***God has revealed those things to us by his Spirit**. The Spirit searches everything, especially **the deep things of God**.*

1Co 2:11 *After all, who knows everything about a person except that person's own spirit? In the same way, **no one** has known everything about God except God's Spirit.* **(GW)**

While on The Cross Jesus said, ((("IT IS FINISHED")))!

Joh 19:28 *Jesus knew that by now everything had been completed; and **in order to make the "scripture" come true**, he said, "I am thirsty"* **(GNB).**

Joh 19:29 *A bowl was there, full of cheap wine; so a sponge was soaked in the wine, put on a stalk of hyssop, and lifted up to his lips.* **(GNB)**

Joh 19:30 *Jesus drank the wine and said, **"It is finished!"** Then he bowed his head and **gave up his spirit*** **(GNB).**

Luk 23:46 *And when Jesus had cried with a loud voice, he said, Father, into thy hands __I commend__ my spirit: and having said thus, he __gave up the ghost__.* **(KJV)**

The WORD Commend means ~~~ To place along side, <u>to deposit</u> as a TRUST for Protection, **to send forth** for **Safe Keeping**.

~~~ Jesus <u>is</u> God, He's eternal, <u>how</u> can HE <u>DIE</u>? ~~~

John 10:18 *No one can kill me without my consent - I __lay down__ my __life voluntarily__. For I have the right an power to __lay it down__ when I want to and also the right and __power to take it again__. For the __Father__ has given me this right"* **(TLB)**

The LIFE that Jesus was referring to was "HIS SPIRIT" - He had The Right and power to separate Himself from the <u>Holy Spirit</u> ~ Which is **LIFE**, and while in Sheol ~ **(The Abode of the Dead)** ~ **He had the right and power to Receive The Holy Spirit Again.** This was recorded in Heaven before the foundation of the world.

(**Word is Father)**", in order to lay his life down He will use **WORDS** ; He gives these **WORDS** in ~~ Luke 23:46 and Jesus cried out in a loud voice, **and said**, "Father, to Thy hands I **entrust my spirit**." And after uttering these **words** He **yielded up His spirit (WNT).**

In the New Testament brother James explains what death is. **James 2:26** *Just as the __body is dead__ when there is __no spirit in it__: The physical body can't move without a spiritual body in it* **(LVB)**!

The Angels came and took Jesus and the criminal to Abraham's Bosom. The Angels didn't take their earthly body to Sheol; but their **SPIRITUAL** Bodies.

In obedience to His own plan that He had before the foundations of the world; He sent His spiritual body back to the father and took on Satan's spiritual body (**serpent on a pole**). That is exactly what happened to the **FIRST ADAM**. Adam lost the glory and now Jesus is getting it back **for all of the redeemed**. Remember one of the criminals that was crucified with Jesus asked Him to remember him. And Jesus **said** unto him, **Luk 23:43** *Verily I say unto thee, __Today__ shalt thou be with me in __paradise__* **(KJV).**

That day Jesus went with him to Abraham's Bosom in **SHEOL**. That was the place that Satan was allowed to keep all the Old Testament **BELIEVERS,** from Adam's time, right up until Jesus showed up.

So what exactly happed then, when "***HE GAVE UP***" His Spirit. The EXACT same thing that happed to ADAM through DISOBEDIENCE; happened to JESUS through OBEDIENCE to The Father. **Joh 10:***17* *For this reason the Father loves me, because I **lay down my life** that I **may take it up again.*** **(ESV)**

Joh 10:18 *No one takes it from me, but **I lay it down of my own accord**. I have authority to lay it down, and I have **authority to take it up again**. This charge **I have received from my Father**.*" **(ESV) And** **WHO** **is HIS** **Father?** ~~~ THE **WORD**!

It says in **Luk 23:46** *And Jesus gave a loud cry and said, Father, into your hands **I give my spirit**: and when he had said this, **he gave up his spirit** **(BBE)**.

Jesus in obedience to "**THE WORDS**" sealed "**IN HEAVEN**", sent His Spiritual Body back to "**THE FATHER**" which is where "**HIS WORDS**" ~ reside Forever ~ Sealed "**In Heaven**".

When Jesus sent His Spirit back to the Father is exactly what happened to Adam in **DISOBEDIENCE.** Adam Lost "**The Glory**" that God gave him when **HE Created Him**, and Adam was given The "**Spiritual Body**" of Satan. Now Adam has "**Fallen From The Glory**".

This is the exact same thing that happened to Adam, ~~~ Adam **FELL FROM** God's "**GLORY**" through Disobedience ~~~ Jesus of His own free will gave up "**THE GLORY**" ~~~ (FOR US) ~~~ Then He took on Satan's Spiritual body **OF SIN**. **2Co 5:21** *For he hath "**made him** to be **sin**" for us, who knew no sin; that we might be made the righteousness of God in him.* **(KJV)**

Chapter 16
~~~ THE SHROUD OF TURIN ~~~

To keep in **complete agreement** with *HIS WORD*, is why we have ~~~~

"**THE SHROUD OF TURIN**," even today.

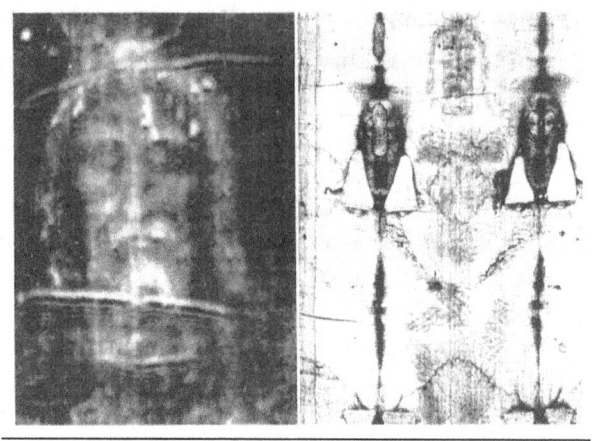

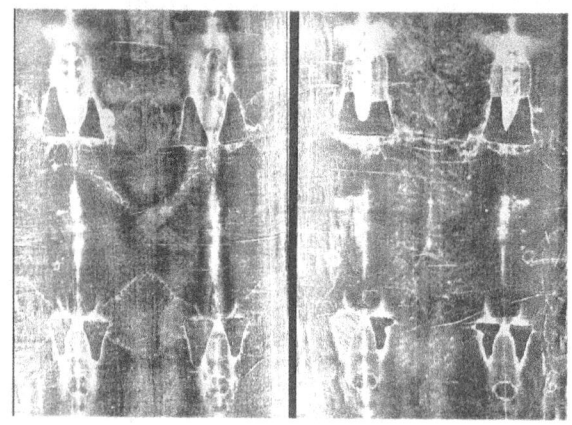

John. 2:19 *Jesus answered and said unto them,*
Destroy this temple,
and in three days I will raise it up **(DRB)** ~~~

This is what has been shown to me about the word (Destroy).

DESTROY - Means:
> to loosen, undo, **dissolve**, anything bound, tied,
> or **compacted together**
> an assembly, i.e. to dismiss, break up to annul,
> subvert to **loose** what is
> compacted or built together , to break up,
> demolish, destroy, to **dissolve something coherent into parts,**
> to destroy metaph., to overthrow, to do away with - **break down**

Jesus had already spoken what would happen to His Body In The Tomb. The Word says in, **1 Cor 6:19** *What? know ye not that your body is the temple of the Holy Ghost which is in you, which ye have of God, and ye are not your own?* **(KJV)** The physical body is (**TEMPORAL**) ~~ but The **Spirit** in the Temporal Body is **Eternal**. Jesus was saying that He was going to **LOOSEN** His physical body to ~~ **DISSOLVING** it into *small parts*.

Jesus' physical body was only (**TEMORARY**) and the "*TEMPORAL CANNOT INHERIT ETERNAL LIFE*"!!! If Jesus raised His **Temporal** body into an **Eternal Body**, Then *Satan has become His Father* because;

Satan could say YOU just violated your "**WORD**" ~~ We all know that is Impossible because, in **Heb 6:18** it says, *"That by two immutable things, in which it was **impossible for God to lie**"* **(KJV).** Jesus has left us **with physical proof** of what happened **in the tomb to His Body**.

(KJV) Gen 3:19 *In the sweat of thy face shalt thou eat bread, till thou **return unto the ground**; for **out of it** wast thou taken: for **dust thou art**, and unto **dust shalt thou return**.*

JESUS DESTROYED
THE BODY OF SIN

All you have to do is to look at "*The Shroud of Turin*). There lies the imprint of "*His Body* "or the "**TEMPLE**" that He *Destroyed*– **Broke Up Into Small Parts**. In **(KJV)2 Cor 4:18**While we look not at the things which are **seen**, but at the things which are **not seen**: for the things which are **seen are temporal**; but the things which are **not seen are eternal.**

Chapter 17
~~ Let's look at how God made Adam ~~

Adam **didn't choose to be here**, he was the First "**Son of God**" to be manifested in the flesh in the *image of God* and in a **Temporal** body. Gods has always known from the beginning that there was going to be **division** in His kingdom, because He Knows **All** Things. Everything we experience will come from His Plan.

When Lucifer Rebelled against **God's Command** for **ALL** The Angels to **Worship ADAM;** this did not take Jesus by surprise!

Heb 1:6 *And again, when **he bringeth** in the*

firstbegotten into the world,~ (Adam) *~ he saith, And
let all the angels of God worship him*. **(KJV)**

(Isa 46:10 *Declaring the end from the beginning)* **(KJV)** - Right now we're dealing with the
in between. ~~ **John 17:24** *Father, I want them with me ~ these you've given me ~ so that
they can see my glory. You gave me the glory because you loved me before the world began*
(LVB). This kingdom stuff started before the world ever was.

Mat 25:34 *Then shall the King say unto them on his right hand, Come, ye blessed of my
Father, inherit the kingdom prepared for you from the "foundation" of the world* **(KJV)**:

The rebellion of God's people started right after God Created The Earth and placed Adam on
it. God has chosen a way to redeem those that had **disobeyed Him**. He chose to create the
heavens and the earth to bring a physical, **temporal**, place to bring about the most perfect
way to bring judgment on the **rebellious ones** that He had to deal with. That's **you and me**;
and **everyone** born on planet earth!

I guess **passing the buck** may have started with God. He has left our eternal estate -
(where we spend eternity), totally **up to each individual**, so he is **not responsible** for anyone
going to hell. He has offered Jesus as **the only way back to God**, if we accept his offer, we
become **one with Him again**. If we **refuse** then His **default** setting will be your abode
forever, serious stuff!!!

2Pe 3:9 *The Lord isn't slow about keeping his promises, as some people think he is. In fact,
God is patient, because he wants everyone to turn from sin and no one to be lost* **(CEV).**

Chapter 18
Now back to how Adam was made.

The only source for that of course is **God's word**, seeing how He was the one who
created him! ~ **Genesis 2:7** *And the Lord God formed man of the dust of the ground, and
breathed into his nostrils the breath of life; and man became a living soul* **(KJV).**

Its so funny to me that several years ago some famous laboratory examined a human
body and found all the **elements of the earth** in it! Do you suppose that **surprised** God???
Chuckle, chuckle. I suppose if they don't know, **they just don't know**. Isn't it amazing that
all of our food comes from the ground **~ DIRT ~** we put seeds in the ground and we have

wonderful things that the **dirt will produce,** potatoes, beans, tomatoes, cucumbers etc.; all come **from the ground**, so all we are eating is **recycled dirt**, amazing.

God made a mud image of himself, then He put **His spiritual body** in it and that pile of mud could move on it's own. We see from the New Testament what a man is comprised of. ~~

James 2:26 *For just as a human body **without a spirit** is lifeless* **(WNT)**. It is the spiritual body inside these vessels of clay that causes the clay to move.

When we look at one another we are **not** seeing the **real person**, we are looking at **clay**. The **real person** is **inside that vessel of clay** and that one **we can't see**, and is **eternal**. The reason you **can't see** it is because it is **eternal**. What is **seen** is only **temporary**, but what is **unseen lasts forever.**

If an ***unsaved person*** gives up his spirit, or shall we say die, that **body of clay** will revert back **to dust**, where it **came from**; but the **real person** that was inside that vessel of clay will be **escorted to hell**, to await **The Great White Throne Judgment**.

Every soul lives **inside** a spiritual body. The **inner man is spiritual**, everyone born on planet Earth has a **Gen. 3:15 corruptible seed**, which is what Jesus referred to in ~~ **John 8:44** *You **are** of your **father the devil**, and your will is to do your **father's desires*** **(GNB).**

The only way **out of** Satan's spiritual kingdom is just what Jesus said, you must be **born from above** ~ or again.

Chapter 19
~~~ AND WHO WAS ADAM? ~~~

Adam was THE "SON OF GOD";
Adam was The "GOD of this World" IN THE FLESH.

Satan Explains to Adam how He was kicked out of Heaven

I found this in the Book of **Enoch**, and HE was **VERY** Close to **God's** Heart!

~~~ **Adam & Eve asks** Satan some Questions! ~~~

Have we taken away thy glory and caused thee to be without honor? Why do you continually harass us, thou enemy (and persecute us) to the death in **wickedness and envy**?"

And with a heavy sigh, the devil spoke: "O Adam! All my hostility, envy, and sorrow ***is for thee*** *since* ***it was for Thee*** *that* ***I was Expelled from my Glory***, which I possessed ***in the heavens*** in the midst of the angels and ***for thee was I cast out*** in the earth." Adam answered, "What do you tell me? What have I done to thee or what is my fault against thee? Seeing that thou hast received no harm or injury from us, why do you pursue us?"

The devil replied, "Adam, what do you tell me? It is for ***thy sake*** that ***I have been hurled from this place.*** When <u>thou was formed</u>. I was hurled out of the presence of God and ***banished from the company of the angels.*** When God blew into you the **breath of life** thy face and ***likeness was made in the image of God,*** Michael also brought ***thee*** and ***made (us)*;** <u>worship thee</u> in the sight of ***God the Lord spake***: Here is ***Adam,*** I have made Him in our image and likeness."

And Michael went out and ***((("called all the angels")))*** saying: ***Worsip the image of God.*** As The <u>Lord hath commanded</u>. And "<u>Michael himself worshipped first</u>"; then he called me and said: "***worship the Image of God the Lord".*** And I answered, "I have no need to worship Adam" And since Michael kept <u>urging me to worship</u>, I said to him, "Why dost thou urge me? I will not worship an inferior and younger being (than I). I am his senior in the creation, *before he was made I was already made*. It's his duty to **worship me**." When the ***angels, who were under me***, heard this, ("***they refused to worship him")***.

And Michael saith, "***Worship The Image of God***!, Michael was giving ***God's COMMAND*** to ***("Worship ADAM")*** but if thou wilt not worship him, the Lord God will be wrath with thee." And I said, "If He be wrath with me, "I will set my seat above the stars (*angels*) of heaven and will be like the Highest."

"Satan speaking" ~~~ And God the Lord was wrath with me banished ("***me and my angels")*** <u>from our glory</u>; and on thy account were we <u>expelled from our abode</u> "***into this world"*** and **hurled on the earth**. And straightway we were overcome with grief, since **we had been spoiled of so great glory**. And ("***we were grieved")*** when ***we saw "thee"*** in *such "joy and luxury"*. And with ***guile I cheated thy wife and caused thee to be expelled through her (doing) from thy joy and luxury***, as I have been <u>driven out out of "**my glory**"</u>.

Now It is my prayer that you can connect these "<u>DOTS</u>" and **"SEE"** with your **Spiritual** eyes "<u>WHERE WE LOST THE GLORY</u>". <u>We are and always have been Eternal Spiritual Beings.</u>

Eph 1:18 *The eyes of your understanding being enlightened; that ye may know what is the hope of his calling, and what the riches of **the glory** of his inheritance in the saints,* **(KJV)**

God's WORD clearly states that we <u>Once Had The Glory</u>; **That We Have All Fallen From The Glory;** and that WE have been **RE-GLORIFIED**; as **HE IS** so **ARE WE** in this world.

      In summary - All that had lived from Adam's time till the cross were <u>looking forward</u> to a Redeemer. All that **obeyed** God's word were by faith **waiting** for salvation. ~~ **Hebrews 11:10** *Abraham did this because he was confidently **waiting for** God to **bring him** to that strong **heavenly city** whose designer and **builder is God*** **(TLB).**

Chapter 20

~~~ Where the Corruptible SEED of DEATH came from ~~~

      Let's look at what God's Word means about **Life & Death** in God's Kingdom. What actually happened to Adam, after being <u>CREATED</u> in **God's** Image, then shortly after he <u>DIES</u>. Yet they didn't bury his body till he was 930 years old.

Gen 5:5 *And all the days that Adam lived were **nine hundred and thirty years***: *and he died* **(KJV)**. ~~ Yet Adam is Very, Very much Alive today in Heaven. We will see where the people that didn't make heaven, where they went, and still many are going there today. As soon as the Church gets out of its four walls, there will be more going to Heaven! Boot us out of the four walls Lord!

~~~ How was Jesus made to be sin for us? ~~~

      Time to hit the book again, (the **only source** of spiritual truth), here we go.

2Co 5:21 *For he hath made him to be sin for us, who knew no sin; that we might be made the righteousness of God in him* **(KJV).**

Isa 28:9 *Whom shall he teach knowledge? and whom shall he **make to understand doctrine?** them that are **weaned from the milk**, and drawn from the breasts.*

Isa 28:10 *For precept must be upon precept, precept upon precept; line upon line, line upon line; here a little, and there a little:* **(KJV)**

What does precept mean?

The meaning is: ~~~ To constitute; **to enjoin**; send a messenger; **to put** or **set in order**. Another connection to this is ~~~ **2 Timothy 2:15** *Do your **best** to present yourself **to God** as one who has passed the test. Be a **worker** who has nothing to be ashamed of. **Interpret the message** of truth **in the proper way**.* **(SEV)** ~~~ Sorry folks, that takes you **and me** completely out of this picture! John made it very, very clear in ~~~ **John 3:27** *John answered and said, A man can **receive nothing**, except **it be given him from** heaven.* **(KJV)** If this message **didn't** come from heaven, then this is just a **waist of time**. But Oh, what **if** it **is**! That puts the ball back in your court doesn't it; **you decide**. The **Holy Spirit** is our Teacher, and **only He** can interpret the **word of Truth**.

~~~ SIN HAS A BODY ~~~

(KJV) *Romans 6:6 Knowing this, that our old man is **crucified with him**, that the **body of sin** might be **destroyed**, that henceforth we should not serve sin* **(KJV).** This **body of sin** is spiritual; we inherited it from **our father**; physically and spiritually. Physically from our earthly parent, our physical father, through his **BLOOD**; and through his **SEED**, (the seed is spiritual). That spiritual seed goes all the back to Adam, which is **CORRUPTIBLE** seed.

Let's look again where the corruptible seed came from. ~~~ **Genesis 3:15** *From now on you and the woman will be enemies, as will **your offspring** and **hers**. You will **strike his heel**, but he will **crush your head"** **(LB).**

Gen 3:15 *And I will put enmity between thee and the woman, and between **thy seed** and **her seed**; it shall bruise thy head, and thou shalt bruise his heel.* **(KJV)**

In verse {15} **Jesus** is speaking to Satan and saying that **He** was going to put hostility ~~~ (**unfriendly**) ~ Spiritual conditions between those born with Satan's spiritual seed ~ in a human being and HER SEED. Now The Seed of the woman can **ONLY** mean Christ; because The Woman doesn't have any SEED, ONLY the Male has SEED. Therefore **HER SEED** can **ONLY** mean **Christ.**

One more time: the woman doesn't carry "The Seed", the male does. The **SEED** that Mary carried, came from The **Holy Spirit**. There was a **BREAK** in The **Blood Line**, "Hallelujah", (That means Praise Jehovah)!!!

Jesus had no earthly father; **no earthly man** had anything to do with being his father. Let's look at the account we have been given in the ~~ **Luke 1:35** *And the angel said to her, "The*

*Holy Spirit will come **upon** you, and the **power** of the Most High will **overshadow** you; therefore **the child** to be born will be **called holy**, the **Son of God**.* **(RV)**

Do you see the **BREAK** in the **BLOOD** line of the **SEED**? Everyone born on planet earth has their **spiritual seed link**, that goes all the way **back to Adam** which is **Corruptible** and **Spiritual**.

Now we can see why Jesus said in ~~~ **John 3:3** *Jesus answered: In all truth I tell you, **no one** can **see** the kingdom of God **without** being **born from above**.* **(NJB)** (Saved, Born Again), however you label it, without receiving the Free Gift of His Spirit, you will be **ETERNALLY SEPARATED** from God. Serious stuff, people! Now, I need to get back on track.

> **A** - First we must establish what **SIN** is:
> > 1. First, it is an **error** of the **understanding**.
> > 2. Sin hinders the **perception** of **TRUTH.**
> > 3. It will cause you **to fail** to hit the **mark.**

> **B** - We need a quick definition of the word **made**:
> > 1. To change one thing **into** another, or, **become something**.
> > 2. When used with a noun it is describing **A PLAN** or course of action, to **perform** it.
> > 3. To point to an **actual result**: To the **scope** and **character of the result**.

Jesus came to restore what the First Adam lost through disobedience. ~~~ **Romans 5:19** *Adam caused many **to be sinners** because he **disobeyed** God, and Christ caused many to be made acceptable to God because he **obeyed**.* **(LB)**

We already know how Adam lost **God's** spiritual body and received **Satan's** spiritual body; that happened through **disobedience**. Now what did Jesus do to be **obedient**, that caused many to be made righteous? The only answer to that is that **HE WAS MADE SIN** for **US**. He took on the **same position** we were in!

Most, if not all of God's word, gives us **Word PICTURES**. If I say the word elephant, in your mind you don't see the letters **E_L_E_P_H_A_N_T!** Do you? No you see the Picture of an elephant. Have you ever heard that a picture can be worth a thousand **WORDS**. Well that's the way God's word is. One such striking example of that is given in **Num 21:8** *Then the LORD told Moses to make a metal snake and put it on a pole, so that anyone who was bitten could look at it and be healed.* **(GNB)**

Every one born on planet earth has been **bitten** by **this serpent!** This serpent is our spiritual father Jesus said, "If you will look to the **CROSS**", and see that I have taken your place; I am taking on Satan's **spiritual body** and am going into Sheol, **(The Abode of The Dead)** in your place. I will **TASTE DEATH** for **everyone**. *I have the keys of hell and of death.* **(KJV)** He went into Sheol for us so we don't have to!

He became **what we "were"**, so we could **become what HE "IS"**!Good place for another "**HALLELUJAH**"!!! ~~ (Praise God) ~~ Let's go back to the truth, **Thy Word** is **Truth!**

Luke 23:46 *And when Jesus had cried with a loud voice, **he said**, Father, into thy hands I **commend my spirit**: and having said thus, he **gave up the ghost*** (KJV).

The **(LVB)** states it this way ~~
Luke 23:*46* *Then Jesus shouted, ``Father, I **commit my spirit** to you," and with **those words** he **died.*** The word **COMMEND** means "To **send forth** for safe keeping.

The other thing Jesus said about His Death was in ~
Joh 10:17 *"The Father loves me because I am willing to **give up my life**, in order that I may **receive it back** again. {18} No one takes my life away from me. I give it up of my own free will. I have the **right to give it up**, and I have the **right to take it back**. This is what my Father* **(THE WORD)** *has commanded me to do."* **(GNB)**

Chapter 21
This is how Jesus became ~~~ The First Born From THE DEAD

Rev 1:5 *And from Jesus Christ, the true witness, **the first to come back from the dead**,*
(BBE)

Our "**BROTHER**" Jesus was ("***BORN AGAIN*** ") in Sheol, THE "**FIRST BEGOTTON** FROM **THE DEAD**". While He was on that Cross He promised that thief hanging beside Him saying in ~ **Luk 23:43** *And Jesus said unto him, Verily I say unto thee, **To day** shalt thou be with me in **paradise**.* **(KJV)**

Jesus did not ascend to Heaven form The Cross.

Eph 4:8 *Wherefore he saith, When he ascended up on high, he __led captivity captive__, __and__ __gave gifts__ unto men. {9} (Now that he ascended, what is it but that he __(also "descended__ __first")__ __into the lower parts of the earth?__ ~~~ (Sheol){10} He that "__descended__"is the same also that "__ascended__" up far above all heavens, that he might fill all things.* **(KJV)**

Just as Jesus had promised that thief on The Cross, that very day he went with Jesus into "**Sheol**", ~ From The Cross ~ into Paradise or **Abraham's Bosom**.

This is the account that is given, of how Jesus **received again** the **spiritual body** that He **commended to** **the Father** while on the **cross**. An archangel is going to deliver God's *word* ~ which is ~ "**THE FATHER**" ~ to Jesus in **Sheol**, where He is being **illegally** held by Satan. ~~~

1 Thessalonians 4:16 *For the Lord Himself will come down from Heaven with a* __loud word of command__*, and with an* __"archangel's voice"__ *and the* __"trumpet of God"__*, and the* __"dead in Christ"__ *will rise* __"first"__ **(WNT).** ~~~ Here's where we have to **"rightly divide"** the **"Word of Truth"**.

And what message did **Gabriel** ~ "SPEAK" ~ to Jesus?

Heb 1:5 *For unto which of the angels said he at any time, ~ Thou art __my Son__, ~ __this day__ have ~ I __begotten thee__? And ~ __again__, I will be to ~ __him a Father__, and ~ __he__ shall be ~* __to me a Son__?

This verse is saying that a **Message from** ~ " **The Father**" ~ "**The WORD**" ~ **Sealed In** **Heaven** ~ is going to be **SPOKEN** by **an archangel** ~ ("**Gabriel**") ~ the **"vocal cords of the** **angel"** is speaking **words** ~ (**WORD IS FATHER**) ~ that are **ordered by God**! The **source** **of The Authority** of the **Words to be Spoken**, are referred to as, "The Lord Himself. **God** and **His WORD** are **one in the same**; you **cannot separate** God **from** His **WORD**!!! ~~ (**Jesus** is **GOD SPEAKING WORDS**).

John 1:1 *In the __beginning__ was the __Word__, and the __Word__ was __with God__,* **(Jesus)** *and the__Word__* __was God__. **(KJV)** The **AUTHORITY** of The Words that are spoken go back to The Lord Himself.

In summary ~ Jesus was **raised from the dead** the **same way** you were raised **from the dead**! While in Sheol, He **received** God's **"word"**, ~ Spoken by "**Gabriel**" and received again the "**Holy Spirit's BODY**".

Psa 16:*10* ~ For thou wilt not leave my soul to **Sheol**, neither wilt thou allow thy Holy One to see corruption. **(DARBY)** ~~~
(Jesus' Body was Completely DESTROYED
before it saw Corruption or Decay!!!)

This verse is referring to "***Jesus' SOUL*** which **is NOW INSIDE SATAN"S SPIRITUAL BODY**."being left in Sheol. Jesus sent HIS <u>SPIRITUAL BODY</u> back to the FATHER through obedience to Gods plan while on The Cross. **Luk 23:46** *And when Jesus had cried with a loud voice, he said, Father, into thy hands I commend my spirit: and having said thus, he gave up the ghost* **(KJV)** . That word <u>COMMEND</u> means to send fourth for safe keeping.

Let's look again at "How **you** were saved", __Born__ Again. ~~ (KJV) 1 **Peter 1:23** *Being **born again**, not of corruptible seed, but of incorruptible, **by the "word of God"**, which liveth and abideth for ever* **(KJV)**. ~~~ God's word is the source of your **spiritual heritage**; obedience to God's word will cause God to move on your behalf!

Chapter 22

~~~ We have been REDEEMED by the blood of God ~~~

Jesus said that our Father was The Devil ~ **John 8:44** *Ye are of your father the devil,* **(KJV)**

We were born in sin according to **Psa 51:5** - *Truly, I was **formed in evil**, and **in sin did my mother give me birth**.* **(BBE)**

Rom 6:1 *What should we say then? Should we continue to sin so that God's kindness will increase?*

Rom 6:2 *That's unthinkable! As far as sin is concerned, **we have died**. So how can we still live under sin's influence?*

Rom 6:3 *Don't you know that all of us who were baptized into Christ Jesus **were baptized into his death?***

Rom 6:4 *When we were baptized into his death, we were **placed into the tomb with him**. As Christ was **brought back from death to life** by the glorious power of the Father, so we, too, should live a new kind of life.*

Rom 6:5 *If we've become united with him in a death like his, certainly we will also be united with him when we come back to life as he did.*

Rom 6:6 *We know that the person we used to be was crucified with him to put an end to sin in our bodies. Because of this we are no longer slaves to sin.*

Rom 6:7 *The person who has died has been freed from sin.*

Rom 6:8 *If we have died with Christ, we believe that we will also live with him.*

Rom 6:9 *We know that Christ, who was brought back to life, will never die again. Death no longer has any power over him.*

Rom 6:10 *When he died, he died once and for all to sin's power. But now he lives, and he lives for God.* **(GW)**

Rom 6:13 *Never offer any part of your body to sin's power. No part of your body should ever be used to do any ungodly thing. Instead, offer yourselves to God as people who have **come back from death and are now alive.** Offer all the parts of your body to God. Use them to **do everything that God approves** of.* **(GW)**

So who was it that rebelled against God and Fell From The Glory that *we **ONCE HAD!*** If you are saved then you have had The Glory ***RENEWED*** ~~~ **Tit 3:5** *Not by works of righteousness which we have done, but according to his mercy he saved us, by the washing of regeneration, and (**"renewing")** of the Holy Ghost;* **(KJV)** ~~~ (re) - means to do again. You cannot ***RE-PAINT*** something - unless it had **been Painted the-first time**.

For ALL have **Sinned** and **Fallen Short** of The ***Glory of God, (which was*** THE HOLY **GHOST**). That's what we lost in the rebellion; and if you are saved you have been ***RE-NEWED*** with The Holy Ghost! That's what *"**re-demption"*** is! Re-deem means to buy back.

Tit 3:5 *Not by works of righteousness which we have done, but according to his mercy he saved us, by the washing of regeneration, and **renewing of the Holy Ghost**;* **(KJV)**

Now in order to <u>RENEW</u> something you had to <u>have it in the first place</u>.

Isa 46:10 *Declaring the end from the beginning, and from ancient times the things that are not yet done, saying, My counsel shall stand, and I will do all my pleasure:* **(KJV)**

Isa 46:10 *"In the beginning, I told you what would happen in the end. A long time ago, I told you things that have not happened yet. When I plan something, it happens. I do whatever I want to do.* **(ERV)**

(Adam)   (Jesus)   (Jesus)   (Adam)

The ~ First ~ shall be ~ Last ~ and The ~ Last ~ shall be ~ First. ~

Mat 20:*16* *So the last will be first, and the first last.* **(BBE)**

Adam before he fell from The GLORY ~
was EXACTLY like ~ ("The Resurrected Christ").
Absolutely no Difference between them.

There

Is

Now

No

Difference between **– The First**

Adam

The

Last

Adam

and

Us

We

Are Now **One**

<u>The ground is level at the foot of "THE Cross"</u>

` This would be a good place to see the **<u>Difference</u>** between The **spirit** of Adam and Eve after **<u>THE FALL</u>**, and The **Spirit** Jesus had.

Gen 3:8 *That evening they heard the LORD God walking in the garden, and they hid from him among the trees.*

Gen 3:9 *But the LORD God* (**Jesus**) *called out to the man, "**Where are you**?"*

Gen 3:10 *He answered, "I heard you in the garden; I **was** **afraid and hid** from you, because **I was naked**."*

Gen 3:11 *(Jesus said) (**"Who"**) told you that you **were naked**?" God asked. "Did you eat the fruit that I told you not to eat?"*

Gen 3:12 *The man answered, "**The woman** you put here with me gave me the fruit, and I ate it."*

Gen 3:13 *The LORD God* (**Jesus**) *asked the woman, "Why did you do this?" She replied, "The snake tricked me into eating it."*

Gen 3:14 *Then the LORD God said to the snake, "You will be punished for this; you alone of all the animals must bear this curse: From now on you will crawl on your belly, and you will have to eat dust as long as you live.*

Gen 3:15 *I* (**Jesus**) *will make **you and the woman hate each other**; her offspring and yours will always be enemies. **Her offspring** (Jesus) will crush your head (Satan), and you will bite **her offspring's heel** (Jesus)."*

Gen 3:16 *And he* (**Jesus**) *said to the woman, "I will increase your trouble in pregnancy and your pain in giving birth. In spite of this, you will still have desire for your husband, yet you will be subject to him."*

Gen 3:17 *And he* (**Jesus**) *said to the man, "You listened to your wife and ate the fruit which **I told you not to eat**. Because of what you have done, the ground will be under a curse. You will have to work hard all your life to make it produce enough food for you.*

Gen 3:18 *It will produce weeds and thorns, and you will have to eat wild plants.*

Gen 3:19 *You will have to work hard and sweat to make the soil produce anything, until you go **back to the soil from which you were formed**. You were made from soil, and **you will become soil again**."* **(GNB)**

This is very interesting that God asked Adam this question; ~

~ *(WHO TOLD YOU THAT YOU WERE NAKED?* ~

Now it is very clear that Jesus **DIDN'T** tell them that they were <u>NAKED</u>. So who told them that they were naked?

This goes back to what The Holy Spirit said to me ~ **SPIRIT IS CONTAINER** ~ The Spirit is the container that your **soul is in**. When God asked ~ "Did you **DO** what I told **YOU** Not To **DO**? That wasn't a surprise to God; He knew that they were going to do that before He placed them on the Earth. The one that told them that **they were naked** was Satan ~ (Their

NEW FATHER). You see it is your **Spirit** that **SPEAKS** to **YOUR SOUL** ~ (which is Your Mind, Your Will, and Your Emotions).

Gen 2:17 *But of the fruit of the tree of the knowledge of good and evil you may not take; for "on the day" when you take of it, **death will certainly come to you*** (BBE).

What happened to them then continues to be a problem for **everyone** born on planet earth **to this** day. They **TRADED FATHER'S**!! ~ **Romans 6:16** *Do you not know that **if you surrender yourselves** as bondservants **to obey any one**, you become the **bondservants** of him whom you obey, whether the bondservants of **Sin** (with **death** as the **result**) or of Duty (resulting in **righteousness**)?* **(WNT)**

So when they **disobeyed their Father ~ (Jesus)**, He said now that you have **chosen** to **obey Satan** instead of **me;** I'll just take **my** spiritual body **back** and give you the **spiritual body** of your **new** father. (Adam and Eve **DIED**, ("Spiritually") ~~ in the "**twinkling of an eye**", eleven one hundreds of a second.) **That's how long it took God to remove His Spirit and give them Satan's spirit - Now they have "FALLEN FROM THE GLORY" of God.** Now they are in a position where they need a Savior! Their only HOPE is **GOD'S GRACE**!!! Can You Relate?

The reverse of what Adam and Eve experienced through Disobedience to their Father is exactly what happened to "JESUS" through obedience to His Father on the cross. He of HIS own choosing sent forth HIS Spirit back to The Father, let's look at what Jesus said.

Luke 23:46 *And when Jesus had cried with a loud voice, he said, Father, into thy hands I commend my spirit: and having said thus, **he gave up the ghost**.* **(KJV)** The word commend, means to send forth for safekeeping.

While Jesus was in Sheol (The Abode of the **Dead**), where all of the old testament Saints were, is where He **RECEIVED** back THE HOLY SPIRIT again.

Rev 1:5 *And from Jesus Christ, who is the faithful witness, and the **first begotten of the dead**, and the prince of the kings of the earth. Unto him that loved us, **and washed us from our sins** in **his own blood**,* **(KJV)**

1Pe 3:18 *For Christ also hath once suffered for sins, the just for the unjust, that he might bring us to God, being put to death in the flesh, but **quickened by the Spirit**:*

1Pe 3:19 *By which also he went and **preached unto the spirits in prison;*** **(KJV)**

1Th 4:*16* *For the Lord himself shall descend from heaven with a shout, with the <u>voice of the</u> <u>archangel</u>, and with the trump of God: and the **<u>dead in Christ</u>** shall rise **<u>first</u>**:*

1Th 4:*17* *Then we which are **<u>alive and remain</u>** shall be **<u>caught up</u>** together with them in the clouds, **<u>to meet the Lord in the air</u>**: and so shall we ever be with the Lord.*

1Th 4:*18* *Wherefore **<u>comfort</u>** one another with these words.* **(KJV)**

  Did you ever stop to think what verse {18} says about ~ **comfort one another** with these words. This should be a great **COMFORT** to **AL**L <u>Christians</u> through understanding what happened to everyone from Adam to The Cross; ~ everyone was taken to Sheol ~ "The Abode of The DEAD" ~ **<u>Including Jesus</u>**.

  2Co 5:8 *So I say that we have confidence. And we really want to be **<u>away from</u>* <u>*this body*</u> *and **<u>be at home with the Lord</u>**.* **(ERV)**

While Jesus was in Sheol ~ in Abraham's bosom ~ **<u>Gabriel</u>** brought this "**<u>WORD FROM</u>** **<u>HEAVEN!</u>**" ~~~ **Heb 1:5** *For to which of the angels did God ever say, "MY SON ART THOU: I **<u>HAVE THIS DAY</u>** BECOME **<u>THY FATHER</u>**;" and **<u>again</u>**, "I WILL **<u>BE A</u>** <u>FATHER</u> TO HIM, AND **<u>HE SHALL BE MY SON</u>**"?* **(WNT)**

  Jesus received AGAIN His Spirit that He had yielded up.
  He had the power to do this because it was written
  so in heaven before the foundation of the wold.

  *We **<u>WERE</u>** Raised FROM **<u>THE DE</u>**AD ~"WITH" ~ HIM!*

  *Col 3:1 Since you <u>were</u> brought back to life **"with Christ"**,* **(GW)**

  We are JOINT heirs WITH Jesus Christ focus on the things that are above-where
  Christ holds the highest position.

From The Resurrection to the end of this age ~ **ALL** ~ That **<u>WERE</u>** made **<u>ALIVE</u>** ~ (Who have Received Jesus' Redemption ~ The ones Born From Above; Everyone with "The Second Birth" when they die ~ **<u>meet the Lord in the air</u>** ~ (IN THE **SPIRIT**) ~

1Pe 3:18 *Christ died once for our sins. An innocent person died for those who are guilty. Christ did this to bring you to God, **when his body was put to death** and **his spirit was made alive.*
 *{19} Christ then **preached to the spirits** that were being **kept in prison.*
(CEV)

The people that were waiting for Jesus to go and preach to the Spirits in prison ~ **(Abraham's Bosom) ~ got emptied out on RESURRECTION DAY!** Now when a redeemed individual dies they go **DIRECTLY** to **HEAVEN!** They do not have to go ~ **"PAST GO",** they don't have time to collect ~ **$200.00 they go directly to Heaven to be with The Lord Forever!**

I find **GREAT Comfor**t in The **TRUTH,** don't **YOU**?

When Jesus Our Brother was raised **From The Dead,** **WE WERE** Raised **WITH HIM**. When a Christian's Spirit leaves his body it only goes to Heaven; if your not saved then your spirit goes to Sheol to await ~ The Second **Resurrection.** ~~ **Rev 20:5** *But the **rest of the dead** lived not again until the thousand years were finished.* **(KJV**

So I find great comfort ~~~ **"KNOWING THE TRUTH"** ~~~ that ALL Christians are **"CAUGHT UP"** to be WITH ~ Jesus ~ when their SPIRIT ~ leaves their Body at DEATH.

Chapter 23
~~~ Where did <u>Our Spirit Man come From?</u> ~~~

Gen 2:7 *And the LORD God formed man of the dust of the ground, and breathed into his nostrils the breath of life; and man became a living soul* **(KJV).** Man became a "LIVING SOUL" ~ because Adam's "SOUL" was inside The "Spirit" of GOD. Our Spirit man came from **HEAVEN.**

We are Eternal Spiritual beings according to ~ **2 Cor 4:18** - *While we look not at the things which are **seen**, but at the things which are **not seen**: for the things which are **seen are temporal**; but the things which are **not seen are eternal**.* **(KJV)**

-

Have you read **Rom 3:23** *<u>All of us</u> have <u>sinned</u> and **fallen** short of God's glory.* **(CEV) It's TIME** to realize where we <u>came</u> **from**, who <u>we</u> **were** then and **WHO** we **ARE NOW**!

We didn't ask to be in any kingdom; we **were** in His kingdom of **LIGHT,** but we came into this world, into a kingdom of **darkness**. Col 1:13 *Who hath delivered us **from the power of darkness**, and **hath translated** us into **the kingdom** of his **dear Son**:* (KJV). You are the only one (with Jesus' help) that can that can get you out of this kingdom of darkness. **Mat 10:28** *And fear not them which kill the body, but are **not able to kill the soul**: but rather fear him which is able to destroy both soul and body **in hell*** (KJV). ~ **Matthew 25: 14** *Then shall he say also unto them on the left hand, Depart from me, ye cursed, into everlasting fire, **prepared** for the **devil and his angels**:*

(Jesus speaking). ~ **John 8:43**. *Why can't you understand what I am saying? It is because you are (**"prevented"**) from doing so! {44} For you are the **children of your father the devil** ; a (**"fallen angel"**) and you love to do the evil things he does. He was a murderer from the beginning and a hater of truth--there is not an iota of truth in him. When he lies, it is perfectly normal; for he is the father of liars. {45}. And so when I tell the **truth**, you just **naturally** don't believe it!* (LVB)

Jesus said that we were born of corruptible seed, which is where we got our spiritual Body from; all the way back to Adam, who lost The Glory before they had ANY children.

1Co 15:44 *The body that is **"planted"** is **a physical** body. When it is **raised**, it will be a **spiritual body**. There is a physical body. So there is also a **spiritual** body.* (ERV)

 Jas 2:26 *For as the **body without the spirit** is dead, so faith without works is dead also.* (KJV)

The only thing that causes your **physical body** to move is **your spiritual body** which is in it. The father of your spiritual body is Satan, **"A FALLEN ANGEL"**!!! ~ If your father is a fallen Angel, so **WHAT** does that infer that you are. I think there is a saying that goes something like this; **Like Father Like son!** Hell was made for **"Satan and his angels."** Just to take this to the next level, let's see what Jesus said would happen in "**The Resurrection**" ~

(Jesus speaking) Luke 20:36 *for neither can they die any more: for they are **equal unto the angels**; and are **sons of God**, being **"sons of the resurrection".*** (ASV) Does this sound like we've been bought back, **redeemed**, restored, and bought with a ransom? ~ "We *WERE* ALL made ONE *AT* THE **RESURRECTION** OF CHRIST."

All of mankind goes back to Adam, and Adam's Father was God; so our roots also go back to God, **Jude 1:6** *And remember the angels who did not keep their place of power but left their proper home. The Lord has kept these **angels in darkness**, bound with **everlasting chains**, to be judged on the great day.* **(NCV)** ～～ "This will take place at The *Second Resurrection.*" ～～

1 Corinthians 6:3 *Know ye not that we shall **judge angels**? How much more things that pertain to this life?* **(KJV)** ～ **Joh 3:18** *__No one__ who has **faith in God's Son** will be **condemned**. But **everyone who doesn't have faith in him** has already been **condemned for not having faith** in God's only Son.* **(CEV)**

Just as a reminder to those who haven't received this thought; our **Spirit and Soul are Eternal** **2 Cor 4:18** *While we look not at the things which are __seen__, but at the things which are __not seen__: for the things which are __seen are temporal__; but the things which are __not seen are eternal.__* **(KJV)**

Eph 2:12 *That's right if you judge yourself for being sinful, not following God's ways; you were without Christ, being aliens from the commonwealth of Israel, and strangers from the covenants of promise, having no hope, and without God in the world* **(KJV).**

If you can make that judgment on yourself, then and only then, can you escape God's judgment, on you. Again you didn't ask to be __in a kingdom__ anyway but; nevertheless you are, if you judge yourself, then you will not be judged of God!

Romans 5:19 *Adam **caused** many to be **sinners** because he **disobeyed** God, and Christ **caused** many to be **made acceptable** to God because he **obeyed**.***(LBV)**

Gal 2:20 *I **have been** crucified with Christ. It is **no longer I** who live, but **__Christ__ __who lives in me.__** And the life I now live in the flesh I live by faith in the Son of God, who loved me and gave himself for me.* **(ESV)**

Php 2:*13* *__God__ is working __in you__ to make **__you willing__ and **able to obey** him.* **(CEV)**

This is the "***ONLY REASON***" why I can write this book, because it is "**HIS SPIRIT**" in me that is doing the writing, **not** ME, **I** DIED **with** Christ.

The simple "**TRUTH"** is that we "**DIED"** with Christ **2000** Years Ago and we "**WERE"** also **"RAISED"** "with **HIM**" **2000** Years Ago.

Col 3:1 *Since you __were__ brought __back__ to life __with__ Christ, focus on the things that are above- where Christ holds the highest positio*n. **(GW)**
Col 3:2 *Set your affection on __things above__, not on things on the earth.*
Col 3:3 *For ye __are dead__, and __your life__ is hid with Christ in God.*
Col 3:4 *When Christ, who is our life, shall appear, then shall __ye also appear with him in glory__.* **(KJV)**

Eph 2:12 *That __at that time__ ye were __without Christ__, being aliens from the commonwealth of Israel, and strangers from the covenants of promise, having no hope, and __without God__ in the world:* **{13}** *But __now in Christ Jesus__ ye who sometimes were far off are made nigh by the blood of Christ.* **(KJV)**

1Jn 3:2 *My dear friends, __we are already God's children__, though what we will be hasn't yet been seen. But we do know that when Christ returns, we will be like him, because we will see him as he truly is.* **(CEV)**

1Jn 3:2 *My dear friends, we __are now__ God's children, but it is not yet clear what we shall become. But we know that when Christ appears, __we shall be like him__, because we shall see him as he really is.*
(GNB)

Chapter 24
~~~ (Spirit is Container) ~~~

Need an interjection here of (Spirit is Container)
On the morning of November 1,1995 @ 4:30 am ~ God spoke to me ~ "in my Spirit"
Three little WORDS
~~~ Spirit is Container ~~~

Translation of that is, your soul is inside your Spirit Man or Inner man. You'll understand that God has made us this way for Separation. As indicated in **Heb 4:12** *For the __word__ of God is quick, and powerful, and sharper than any two edged sword, piercing even to the __dividing asunder__ of __soul and spirit__.* **(KJV)** On can learn that by this process Jesus could DIE and then be RAISED from the DEAD. We have a SOUL which Lives in a Spiritual Body and our Spiritual Body Lives in a Physical Body. **1 Co 15:44** *It is sown a natural body; it is raised a spiritual body. There is a __natural body__, and there is a __spiritual body__.* **(KJV)**

Jesus had a Natural "Temporary "body; ~ inside that **Temporary** body was a **SPIRITUAL BODY** that was **ETERNAL** and came From His **Father** ~ THE **WORD** .

Inside Jesus' SPIRITUAL Body was His **SOUL**. God's **WORD** has the ability to **"seperate"** the SOUL from the SPIRITUAL Body as stated in **Heb 4:12** *For the word of God is living and full of power, and is sharper than any two-edged sword, cutting through and **making a division** even of the **soul and the spirit**, the bones and the muscles, and quick to see the thoughts and purposes of the heart*. **(KJV)**

Ps 16:10 *For thou wilt not leave my **soul** to Sheol; neither wilt thou suffer thine holy one to see corruption*. **(RV)** ~~~ This verse is referring to "***Jesus' SOUL*** "being left in Sheol. Jesus sent HIS SPIRITUAL BODY back to the FATHER through obedience to Gods plan while on The Cross. **Luk 23:46** *And when Jesus had cried with a loud voice, he said, Father, into thy hands I commend my spirit: and having said thus, he gave up the ghost* **(KJV)** . That word **COMMEND** means to send fourth for safe keeping.

Your **SOUL** resides (((("**INSIDE**")))) Your **Spirit** ~ Remember "Spirit is Container". When Jesus ***Commended*** His SPIRIT back to the Father ~ **NOW** Jesus' **SOUL** is in Satan's Spiritual Body. ~~~ That is why it says in ~ **Psa 16:10** *For You will not leave My **soul** in" Sheol"; You will not give Your Holy One to see corruption*. **(LITV)**

The Holy Spirit never went to Sheol With Jesus. Jesus had taken on The "**EXACT**" Same Spirit that **we were born** with the **first time,** ~ Satan's Spirit; in order to get into **SHEOL ~ LEGALLY**.

　　　　Sheol was the abode of the DEAD. Everyone from Adam to the Cross ~ "Including JESUS"
went to Sheol as a **captive of Satan**; this was God's plan "before" He Created Adam. ~ **1Co 2:8** *The rulers of this world didn't know anything about this wisdom. If they had known about it, they would not have nailed the glorious Lord to a cross.* **(CEV)**

When God made the Earth He incorporated Hell or **Sheol** in the middle of the Earth **before** He put Adam on it. **Isa 46:10** *Declaring the end from the beginning, and from ancient times the things that are not yet done, saying, My counsel shall stand, and I will do all my pleasure*: **(KJV)**

Isa 46:10 *"In the beginning, I told you what would happen in the end. A long time ago, I told you things that have not happened yet. When I plan something, it happens. I do whatever I want to do.* **(ERV)**

In summary ~ Jesus was **raised from the dead** the **same way** you were raised **from the dead**! While in Sheol, He **received** God's **word**, and received again the **Holy Spirit's BODY**. Let's look again at "How **you** were saved", **Born** Again. ~ 1 **Peter 1:23** *Being **born again**, not of corruptible seed, but of incorruptible, **by the word of God,** which liveth and abideth for ever.* **(KJV)** God's word is the source of your **spiritual heritage**; obedience to God's word will cause God to move on your behalf!

~~~ We are **BORN AGAIN** by His **WORD** . ~~~

Jas 1:18 *He wanted us to be **his own special people**, and so **he sent the true message** to give us new birth.* **(CEV)**

Jas 1:18 *By his own will **he brought us into being** through **the word of truth**, so that we should have first place among all his creatures.* **(GNB)**

(KJV) 1 Peter 1:23 *Being **born again**, not of **corruptible seed**, but of **incorruptible,** by the **word of God**, which liveth and abideth for ever.* The **(LBV)** says it this way ---

1 Peter 1:23 *For you have a new life. It was **not passed** on **to you** from your **parents**, for the life they gave you will **fade away**. This **new one** will last **forever**, for it comes **from Christ**, God's ever-living **Message** to me*n. ~ **(WNT)** ~ **Romans 8:11** *And if the **Spirit of Him** who **raised up Jesus** from the **dead** is dwelling **in you**, He who raised up Christ from the dead will **give Life** also to your mortal bodies because of **His Spirit** who dwells **in you**.*

And it goes right back to **John 6:63**, *the ~ **words** ~ that I speak unto you, they are ~ **spirit**,~ and they **are life**.* **(KJV)** Jesus was "**The *First Born* from the Dead**," by the **WORD** of God, and you can be **Born Again** by the **Word of God!!**

Rev 1:5 *and from Jesus Christ the faithful witness, the "**firstborn of the dead"**,* **(ESV)**

We could go on and on about the **WORD**; it's a lamp unto my feet and a light to my path; but sufficient unto the cause is that which has been expounded on, right!!!

Chapter 25
~~~ Whose Spirit are YOU FROM? ~~~

Jesus brought this subject up by saying in ~~~ **Luk 9:55** *But He turned and rebuked them and said, You **do not know** of **what spirit you are**.* **(MKJV)**

Joh 12:48 *He that __rejecteth me__, and __receiveth not my words__, hath one that judgeth him:* __the word__ *that I have spoken, the same shall judge him in the last day.* **(KJV)**

Chapter 26
~~~ Where did we come from ~ Who are we? ~~~

1) We are Eternal **Spirit beings.** - **2 Cor 4:18**
2) We all were in **Adam.** - **1 Cor 15:22**
3) All saved are in The **Last Adam.** - **1 Cor 15:22**
4) Adam was the **son of God.** - **Luk 3:38**
5) Then we were **sons of God before Adam was. (RDV)**
6) For all have fallen short of **God's Glory.** - **Rom 3:23**
7) If you are saved then **you have been Glorified. Rom 8:29**
8) You have received "__The Renewal of The Holy Spirit__ that Adam lost. **Tit 3:5**
    a) You cannot be RENEWED with something "unless," YOU had it in the
        first place. Renew means to do **AGAIN**.

__All Spiritual beings__ that God made in the beginning of eternity were "**SONS OF GOD**".

1) "__Sons of God__" saw the daughters of men were fair. ~ **Gen 6:2**

2) Job 2:1 again there was a day when the "sons of God" came to present
    themselves before the Lord. **(BBE)** ~ We were a part of that group. ~

Job 38:7 *When the morning stars sang together, and all the "__sons of God__" shouted for joy?*

Joh 1:12 *But as many as received him, to them gave he power to become the "__sons of God__",* even *to them that believe on his name:*

Rom 8:14 *For as many as are led by the Spirit of God, they are the "__sons of God__".*

Rom 8:19 *For the earnest expectation of the creature waiteth for the manifestation of __the "sons of God".__*

Php 2:15 *That ye may be blameless and harmless, the "__sons of God__", without rebuke, in the midst of a crooked and perverse nation, among whom __ye shine as lights__ in the world;*

1Jn 3:1 *Behold, what manner of love the Father hath bestowed upon us, that we should be called the "**sons of God**": therefore **the world knoweth us not**, because it knew him not.*

1Jn 3:2 *Beloved, **now are we** the "**sons of God**", and it doth not yet appear what we shall be: but we know that, when he shall appear, **we shall be like him**; for we shall see him as he is.* **(KJV)**

3) Mat 25:41 *Then shall he say also unto them on the left hand, Depart from me, ye cursed, into everlasting fire, prepared for the **devil and his angels**:* **(KJV)**

a) Nowhere in scripture does it say that man would go to hell or heaven.
     Only Jesus' **Brothers and Sisters** go to heaven and they are called Saints.

b) Only "The Devil and "HIS ANGELS" go to hell".

             .

Chapter 27
~~~ Where did Satan get His Angels ~~~

Have you ever wondered where Satan got his angels? I have for at least 30 years; then on December 14, 2015 My Father **REVEALED** to me how Satan got his Angels.

Satan got his angels after God gave the message to Michael that ((("**ALL THE ANGELS**"))) must **WORSHIP ADAM** who was "**The Image of GOD**".

After God gave this command then ((("**ALL THE ANGELS**"))) had to make a choice to obey God and ((("WORSHIP ADAM"))) ~ (The Image of God) ~ or DISOBEY God; two thirds of (("THE ANGELS"))) OBEYED God and ((**"WORSHIPED ADAM"**))); BUT one third of the Angels agreed with Satan and **REFUSED** to **WORSHIP ADAM** ~ (The Image of God).

That is where we "**LOST The GLORY**" and Satan became "**OUR FATHER**".
Rev 12:9 *And the great dragon was cast out, that old serpent, called the* **Devil, and Satan,** *which deceiveth the whole world: he was cast out **into the earth, and his angels were cast out ((("with him"))).***

Now it should make more sense why Jesus said in **Mat 25:41** *Then shall he say also unto them on the left hand, Depart from me, ye cursed, into everlasting fire, prepared for the ((("**devil and his angels**")))* **(KJV).** Jesus also said in **Joh 8:44** *You are **the children of your***

father, the Devil, _and you want to follow your father's desires. From the very beginning he was a murderer and_ _has never been on the side of truth,_ **(GNB**

Jesus said in **Jn 8:44** that Satan was our father from our **FIRST BIRTH**, all that are Born **THE SECOND** Time have **Jesus** as their **Father**. In the First birth as a human being, we received Satan's spirit through our natural father, ~ All Born Twice are like God's Angels by receiving God's Spirit through our Heavenly Father which is "The **Word of God**". **Mat 22:30** _For in the resurrection they neither marry, nor are given in marriage, but are_ (**_as the angels of God_**) _in heaven._ **(KJV)**

    Col 3:1 **_Since you ((("were"))) brought back to life ((("with Christ"))),_** _focus on the things that are above ~ where Christ holds the highest position._ **(GW)**

Heb 1:6 And again, when he bringeth in the firstbegotten into the world, he saith, And let all the angels of God worship him. **(KJV)**

Satan Refused to Worship The Image of God and one Third of The Angles agreed with him ~ That's where he got his Angels.

Adam's Soul represented by - Soul

Adams Spirit represented by the Dotted Line

Adams Flesh represented by the solid line

Adam's "GLORIFIED Body" ~~~ "Before The Fall"

Adam was "The God of This World" in the Flesh

1Co 15:44 It is sown a natural body; it is raised a spiritual body. There is a natural body, and there is a spiritual body. **(KJV)**

God's grace has been in effect ALL along through the ages, from creation through till the second coming of Christ. The angels that agreed with Satan to not ((("WORSHIP ADAM"))) have been given a ((("SECOND OPTION"))); every ANGEL that agreed with Satan will have to be born of the water of the womb. **Joh 3:5** *Jesus answered, Verily, verily, I say unto thee, Except a man be **born of water** and **of the Spirit**, he cannot enter into the kingdom of God.* **(KJV)** ~

The water that Jesus referred to there is the **Water of The Womb**; that means that a person is born with a natural physical body which is also a **TEMPORARY** body and inside that physical body is an ETERNAL Spiritual Body; and inside that Spiritual Body is their SOUL.

All of Satan's Angels will be given a **Choice AGAIN** to be **BORN ANEW and RETURN** Back To God. That's what Christians have done as outlined in **John 1:12** ~ *But all who have **received Him**, to them ~ that is, to those who trust in His name ~ He has given the privilege of **becoming children of God**;* **(WNT)**

Jesus said in **John 3:6-7** *Flesh and blood give birth to flesh and blood, but the **Spirit gives birth to things that are spiritua**l. {7} ~ Don't be surprised when I tell you **that all of you must be born from above."** **(GW)**

Jud 1:6 And the angels which kept not their first estate, but left their own habitation, he hath reserved in everlasting chains **under darkness** unto the judgment of the great day. **(KJV)**

**That Darkness can be summed up by saying that
if God has not given you "HIS LIGHT" on a matter
then ~ you will probably never know.**

Chapter 28
~~~ Know ye not that we shall judge angels? ~~~

You are Judging an Angel by ASKING for ~ Another Father. Everyone of **"THE STRANGERS"** including **YOU** that you entertain are Spiritual Beings that "**ORIGINALLY** "came **"FROM HEAVEN".** ~
~~~ **These are JESUS' WORDS** ~~~

(Psa 82:6 (*"**I have said")**, **Ye are gods**; and **all** of you **are children of the Most High**).

Joh 10:35 *If __he called them ("gods,__") unto whom __the word__ of God came, and the __scripture "Cannot" be broken;__* **(KJV)**

Heb 6:18 *That by two immutable things, in which it was __impossible for God to lie__, we might have a consolation, who have fled for refuge to __lay hold upon the hope__ set before us:* **(KJV)**

Note: __If__ Satan __COULD__ catch God in __ONE__ little __LIE__;
Then Satan would become Jesus' Father ~~~
Because Jesus said that "Satan was the
FATHER of ALL LIARS".

Joh 10:33 *They answered, "We do not want to stone you because of any good deeds, but because of __your blasphemy__! You are __only a man__, but you are trying to make yourself __God__!"* **(34}** *Jesus answered, "It is written in your own Law that __God said__, __"You are gods__." {35} We know that what the scripture says is __true forever__; and __God called those people gods__, the people to whom __his message was given__.* **(GNB)**

Every person born on planet Earth has Satan as their Eternal Father; by God's ordinance. If you leave planet earth when you die and you haven't Received Jesus for Your "New Father" ~ Then you will spend ETERNITY with your present Spiritual Father.

Jesus said that our Father was **"THE DEVIL"**, and that we **NEEDED** to be **"BORN FROM ABOVE"**, in order for **"GOD TO BE OUR FATHER"**.

Mat 25:34 *Then shall the King say unto them on his right hand, Come, ye blessed of my Father, inherit the kingdom prepared for you __from the foundation of the world__:* **(KJV)**

Eph 1:4 *According as he hath chosen us in him __before the foundation of the world__, that we should be holy and without blame before him in love:* **(KJV)**

Heb 4:3 *For we which have believed do enter into rest, as he said, As I have sworn in my wrath, if they shall enter into my rest: although the works were __finished from the foundation of the world__.* **(KJV)**

Rev 13:8 *And all that dwell upon the earth shall worship him,* **whose names are not written in the book of life of the Lamb** *slain from the foundation of the world.* **(KJV)**

These are the people who are

willing to receive the

MARK OF THE BEAST

In His Forehead or

In His Hand

Rev 14:11 *And the smoke of their torment ascendeth up for ever and ever: and they have no rest day nor night,* **who worship the beast and his image**, *and* **whosoever receiveth the mark of his name.** **(KJV)**

Rev 16:2 *And the first went, and poured out his vial upon the earth; and there fell a noisome and grievous sore upon the men which had the* **mark of the beast**, *and upon them which worshipped his image.* **(KJV)**

Rev 20:4 *And I saw thrones, and they sat upon them, and judgment was given unto them: and I saw* **the souls of them that were beheaded for the witness of Jesus**, *and for the word of God, and which* **had not worshipped the beast, neither his image, neither had received his mark upon their foreheads, or in their hands;** *and they* **lived and reigned with Christ** *a thousand years.* **(KJV)**

Can you make the connection that we all "**came from**" Heaven before the world ever was. We *were* The Sons of God that rebelled with Satan ~~~ **John 8:44** Jesus said that our Father was The Devil.

 2 Cor 4:18 says that our **Spirit is Eternal** and **so is our soul**, because we cant **SEE** them.

Titus 3 :5 says **(KJV)** *Not by works of righteousness which we have done, but according to his mercy he saved us, by the* washing of regeneration, *and ("*renewing*") of the* Holy Ghost; **(KJV)**

(KJV) *Who are kept by the power of God through faith unto salvation*

Folks it is impossible to (**"RENEW"**) anything without it being **_NEW_** in the first place!

**You know one reason why Hell
is going to be so cruel hateful,
damning, condemning!**

Because they were given the same option that we were.

They refused the <u>FREE GIFT OF SALVATION</u>

**Which is Eternity in Total Happiness ~~~
beyond our present imagination! Now that
they find themselves in Hell for ETERNITY ~~~
never being able to escape ~ all they will do for eternity is
HATE THEMSELVES FOREVER !!!!
For refusing such a GIFT**

This is <u>WAY ~ way BEYOND</u> sad.

I can see Romans 12:2 building up!!!

And what does **Romans 12:2** say ~ *And be not conformed to this world: but be ye* **_<u>transformed</u>_** *by the (****"<u>renewing</u>"****) of your mind, that ye may prove what is that good, and acceptable, and <u>perfect, will of God</u>* **(KJV)**.

~~~ RE_NEW ~~~

1) How can you **RE**PAINT a house or car or anything unless it had already been painted <u>in the first place.</u>

2) You can't **RE**NEW your license unless you <u>have one already</u>.

3) There comes a point in time when WE get our minds **RENEWED** by THE ("***WORD")***
OF **GOD.**

Chapter 29
~~~ It is time to review ~~~

I suspect that you came from your father, as did I! My father came from his father and his father came from his father -etc. ~ and it goes in that cycle all the way back to Adam. So where did Adam come from? **Luke 3:38** *Which was the son of Enos, which was the son of Seth, which was the son of Adam, **which was the <u>son of God.</u>** (KJV).*

Where did this Son of God come from? Certainly God's son came from Heaven; His Spirit and Soul were Eternal. The ancestry of everyone born planet earth eventually goes all the way back to Adam ~ **1Co 15:22** *For as in Adam **<u>all die</u>**, even so in Christ shall **<u>all be made alive</u>** . (KJV)* ~ Adam <u>was the Son of God</u>; therefore **we "were" Sons of God also.** We were Sons of God before the fall. **Rom 5:10** *for if, when **<u>we were enemies</u>**, we were <u>reconciled to God</u> by the death of his Son, much more, **<u>being reconciled</u>**, we shall be saved by his life* **(KJV).**

In Jesus' plan of things, He and ONLY He
established The Plan which included ~

Eph 1:4 *Even before the world was made, God had already chosen us to be his through our **<u>union with Christ</u>**, so that we would be holy and without fault before him. Because of his love {5} God had already decided that through Jesus Christ he would **<u>make us his children</u>** ~ this was his **<u>pleasure and purpose</u>**.* **(GNB)**

We weren't reconciled to man; but **To God** who is our "**FATHER**". The word reconciled means, "to receive into ones favor, or to recover God's favor." **Rev 5:9** *And they sung a new song, saying, Thou art worthy to take the book, and to open the seals thereof: for **<u>thou wast slain</u>**, and **<u>hast redeemed</u>** us **<u>to God</u>** by thy blood out of every kindred, and tongue, and people, and nation* **(KJV).**

Redeemed means to buy back*:*
We had to <u>be with God</u>
in the beginning to

**make it possible
to be
bought back**.

Chapter 30

~~~ Have you ever wondered what that Scripture meant in ~~~

Psa 82:1 *A Psalm of Asaph. God standeth in the congregation of the mighty; he judgeth among the gods.*

Psa 82:2 *How long will ye judge unjustly, and accept the persons of the wicked? Selah.*

Psa 82:3 *Defend the poor and fatherless: do justice to the afflicted and needy.*

Psa 82:4 *Deliver the poor and needy: deliver them from the hand of the wicked.*

Psa 82:5 *They know not, neither will they understand; **they walk on in darkness**: all the foundations of the earth are out of course.*

(Psa 82:6 *(**"I have said"**), **Ye are gods**; and **all** of you **are children** of the Most High*).

Psa 82:7 *But **ye shall die like men, and fall** like one of the princes.*

Psa 82:8 *Arise, O God, judge the earth: for thou wilt inherit all nations.* **(Webster)**

Joh 10:34 *Jesus answered them,*
*Is it not **written in your law**,*
*(**"I said"**), (**"Ye are gods"**)* (KJV)

Joh 10:35 *If **he called them (**"**gods**,*"*) unto whom **the word** of God came, and the* **scripture**
"Cannot" be broken; *(KJV)*

John 10:35 *You can't argue with the Scriptures, and **God spoke to those people** and **called them gods.*** **(CEV)**

Heb 6:18 *That by two immutable things, in which it was **impossible for God to lie**, we might have a strong consolation, who have fled for refuge to lay hold upon the hope set before us:* **(KJV)**

1 Cor 6:3 ***Is it not certain** that we are to be the "**judges of angels**"? how much more then of the things of this life?* **(BBE)**

Everyone that has ever been born on planet Earth or ever will be; is one of *__God's Sons__*.

Heb 13:2 *Be not forgetful to entertain strangers: for thereby some have entertained angels unawares.* **(KJV)**

You cannot move around in this Earth **WITHOUT an EARTH SUIT** with an **ETERNAL SPIRIT** in it.

**For it to be possible to <u>Gain Heaven</u>
Everyone <u>born on planet Earth</u>
has <u>to Born Again</u>
From
<u>Heaven.</u>**

Everyone that has ever lived on planet Earth is a creation of Jesus Christ; and he is The One who Created our Spirit Man that lives inside of us, that can't be seen with our natural eyes. We are ALL Spiritual Beings FIRST ~ Trapped inside our physical body that can be seen.

Eph 2:*10* *For we are **__his workmanship, created__** in Christ Jesus unto good works, which God hath before ordained that we should walk in them.*

Eph 3:9 *And to make all men see what is the **__fellowship of the mystery__**, which from the beginning of the world hath __been hid in God__, who **__created all things by Jesus Christ__***

Eph 4:24 *And that **__ye put on__** **__the new man__**, which after God is **__created in righteousness__** and **__true holiness.__***

Col 1:16 *For by him were **__all things created__**, that are **__in heaven__**, and **__that are in earth__**, **__visible__** and **__invisible__**, whether they be thrones, or dominions, or principalities, or powers: all things **__were created by him__**, and for him:*

Rev 10:6 *And sware by him that liveth for ever and ever, who created heaven, and the things that therein are, and the earth, and the things that therein are, and the sea, and the things which are therein, that there should be time no longer:* **(KJV)**

Chapter 31
~~~ The Father of THE WORD ~~~

Seeing that "**THE FATHER**" is the **ONLY ONE** that knows of Christ's return let's see what The **Father** tells us! In order to do that we will have to go to The ~~~ **"WORD"** ~~~

The ninth chapter of **Daniel** Is what Jesus referred to in **Mat 24:15**! Everyone should find this passage of scripture so **exciting**, so **profound**, to understand what, ~ "**God has Said**"! ~

Histories Greatest **PROPHECY REVEALS** how the **last seven years** on planet Earth ~ **Starts** and **ends**.

~~~ Jesus is Speaking ~~~

Mat 24:15 *"Daniel the prophet spoke about 'the terrible thing **that causes destruction**.' You will see this terrible thing **standing in the holy place**." (**You who read this should understand what it means.***) (ERV)

Dan 11:31 *The northern king will send his army to do terrible things to the **Temple in Jerusalem**. They will **stop the people from offering the daily sacrifice**. Then they will do something really terrible. They will set up that terrible thing **that causes destruction**.* (ERV)

Pro 25:2 *It is the glory of God to "**keep a thing secret**:" but the "**glory of kings**"is to have it (((((("searched out.")))))* (BBE)

I might add that it took me 31 years of SEARCHING to be able to pen these WORDS.

Seeing that The **WORD** is **FATHER** ~ Let's look at what The **Father** has to say about Christ's **SECOND COMING**.

1) Mat 24:3 *As Jesus was sitting on the Mount of Olives, his disciples came to him privately and said, "Tell us, when will this happen? What will be the sign that you are coming again, and when will the world come to an end?" ~ {4} Jesus answered them, "**Be careful not to let anyone deceive you. {5}** Many will come using my name. They will say, 'I am the Messiah,' and they will deceive many people. {6} "You will hear of wars and rumors of wars. Don't be alarmed! These things must happen, but they don't mean that the end has come. {7} Nation will fight against nation and kingdom against kingdom. There will be famines and earthquakes in various places. {8} All of these are only the beginning pains of the end.* (GW)

2) Mat 24:9 *"Then they will **hand you over** to those who will **torture and kill you**. All nations will hate you **because you are committed** to me. {10} Then **many will lose***

*faith. They will **betray and hate each other**. {11} Many **false prophet**s will appear and **deceive many** people. {12} And because there will be **more and more lawlessness**, **most people's love will grow cold**. {13} But the **person who endures to the end** will be saved.* **(GW)**

3) Mat 24:14 *And this gospel of the kingdom shall be **preached in all the world** for a witness unto **all nations**; and **then shall the end come**. {15} When **ye therefore shall see the abomination of desolation**, spoken of **by Daniel the prophet**, stand in the holy place, (**whoso readeth**, let **him understand**:) {16} Then let them which be in Judaea flee into the mountains: {17} Let him which is on the housetop not come down to take any thing out of his house: {18} Neither let him which is in the field return back to take his clothes. {19} And woe unto them that are with child, and to them that give suck in those days! {20} But pray ye that your flight be not in the winter, neither on the sabbath day: {21} For then **shall be great tribulation**, such as was **not since the beginning of the world to this time,** no, nor ever shall be. {22} And except those days should be shortened, **there should no flesh be saved**: ~ **but** for the ~ **elect's sake** ~ those days **shall be shortened**.* **(KJV)**

4) Mat 24:23 *"At that time don't believe anyone who tells you, 'Here is the Messiah!' or 'There he is!' {24} False messiahs and **false prophets will appear**. They will work spectacular, **miraculous signs and do wonderful things to deceive**, if possible, even those whom God has chosen. {25} Listen! I've told you this before it happens. {26} So if someone tells you, 'He's in the desert!' don't go out looking for him. And don't believe anyone who says, 'He's in a secret place!' {27} The **Son of Man** will **come again** just as **lightning flashes from east to west.***

5) Mat 24:29 *And immediately after the tribulation of those days, the **sun shall be darkened** the **moon shall not give her ligh**t and **the stars shall fall from heaven** and the **powers of heaven** shall be moved. {30} And then shall appear the sign of the Son of man in heaven. And then shall all tribes of the earth mourn: and they shall see the Son of man coming in the clouds of heaven with much power and majesty. {31} And he shall send his angels with a trumpet and a great voice: and they **shall gather together his elect** from the **four winds**, from the **farthest parts of the heavens** to the utmost bounds of them.* **(DRB)**

6) Mat 24:32 *"Let the fig tree teach you a lesson. When its branches become green and tender and it starts putting out leaves, you know that summer is near. {33} In the same way, when you see all these things, you will know that the time is near, ready to begin. {34} Remember that all these things will happen before the people now living have all died. {35} Heaven and earth will pass away, but my words will never pass away. {36} "**No one** knows, however, when that day and hour will* come---neither the angels in heaven nor the Son; the **_Father_** """"_alone_"""" _knows_. **(GNB)**

7) Mat 24:37 _The coming of the Son of Man will be **like what happened in the time of Noah**. {38} In the days before the flood people ate and drank, men and women married, up to the very day Noah went into the boat; {39} yet **they did not realize** what was happening until the flood came and <u>swept them all away</u>. That is how it will be when the Son of Man comes._**(GNB)**

8) Mat 24:40 _At that time two men will be working in a field: one will be taken away, the other will be left behind. {41] Two women will be at a mill grinding meal: one will be taken away, the other will be left behind. {42} Watch out, then, because you do not know what day your Lord will come._ **(GNB)**

9) Mat 24:44 _So then, you also must always be ready, because the Son of Man will come at an hour when you are not expecting him. {45} <u>"Who, then, is a faithful and wise servant</u>? It is the one that his master has placed in charge of the other **servants to give them their food at the proper time. {46}** How happy that servant is if his master finds him doing this **when he comes** home! {47} Indeed, I tell you, the master will put that servant in charge of all his property. {48} But if he is a bad servant, he will tell himself that his master will not come back for a long time, {49} and he will begin to beat his fellow servants and to eat and drink with drunkards. {50} Then that servant's master will come back one day when the servant does not expect him and at a time he does not know. {51} The master will cut him in pieces and make him share the fate of the hypocrites. There he will cry and gnash his teeth._ **(GNB)**

Our Heavenly Father has a **plan**. And he wants to **reveal** that plan to whom he chooses. **(KJV) Deuteronomy 29:29** _The secret things belong unto the LORD our God: but those things which are **revealed** belong unto us and to **our children** for ever, that we may do **all** the words of this law._ **(KJV)**

Let's take a closer look at the nine sections mentioned above.

1) Jesus says don't let any one **DECEIVE** You.
    A) He mentions wars and rumors of wars, don't be alarmed.
    B) There will be famines and earthquakes in various places.

2) Many will **loose their Faith**; betray and hate each other.
    A) more and more lawlessness.
    B) Most peoples love will grow cold.

C) <u>**He who endures**</u> to the end will be saved. **(Christians are the only ones SAVED.)**

3) This Gospel (of <u>**GOOD NEWS**</u>) shall be preached to ALL The World.
    A) This scripture should be fulfilled in a few years ~

This is a quote from the Billy Graham Organization.

 "Recently, at meetings in Orlando, Fla., organized by the Billy Graham Center at Wheaton College, it was announced that the <u>**world could be only 10 or 15 years away**</u> from seeing the Great Commission fulfilled".

B) The gospel <u>**HAS**</u> to be preached to all the world <u>**BEFORE**</u> The End Can Come.

C) Jesus refers to the <u>**Abomination of Desolation**</u> ~~ <u>**Spoken**</u> by the prophet <u>**Daniel.**</u>

1) Before The <u>**Abomination of Desolation**</u> can take place The peace treaty has to be signed by the anti-Christ. ~

2) There is going to be <u>**1290 days**</u>, or 3 ½ years <u>**FROM**</u> the time the <u>**peace treaty**</u> is ~ ("*__signed__*") ~ "<u>**UNTIL**</u>" ~ the daily <u>**sacrifice**</u> is taken away.

3) <u>**From**</u> the time the daily sacrifice is taken away, ~ ("<u>**UNTIL**</u>") ~ the abomination that maketh desolate is set up will be **1290** <u>**days**</u>, or 3 ½ years.

4) That means there will be **2580** days ~ or <u>**7 years**</u> from the day that The Peace Treaty is ~ ("signed") ~, Until the Abomination of Desolation takes place.

4) *False messiahs and* **false prophets** *will appear* and do spectacular <u>**signs and wonders to deceive**</u> if possible even the elect.

5) 29 And immediately after the tribulation of those days, the <u>**sun shall be darkened**</u> the <u>**moon shall not give her ligh**</u>t and <u>**the stars shall fall from heaven**</u> and the <u>**powers of heaven**</u> shall be moved.
A) Notice that it says ~ All hell is going to break loose <u>**after the tribulation**</u> of those days.

B) When Satan stands in The Holy Place to declare that he is god ~ this is the <u>**Abomination of Desolation**</u> that Jesus referred to.

C) *And then shall appear the sign of the Son of man in heaven.*

D) And he will send out his angels with a loud trumpet call, and they will gather his elect together from the four winds, from *one* end of heaven to the *other* end of it.

6) *In the same way, when you see all these things, you will know that the time is near, ready to begin.*

A) The generation that sees Israel become a nation; will not all die before all of this is completed.
     1) Israel became a Nation on **May 14,1948**

B) Heaven and Earth shall pass away, but **My WORDS** will **Never** Pass Away.
1) Jesus' WORDS are forever SEALED in Heaven.

Psa 119:89 LAMED. *For ever, O LORD, thy word is settled in heaven.* **(KJV)**

7) *The coming of the Son of Man will be **like what happened in the time of Noah**.*

A) *Yet **they did not realize** what was happening until the flood came and **swept them all away.***
1) Next logical question should be; **WHO** was **taken away** and **WHO** was **LEFT BEHIND**?

2) Correct me if I'm wrong ~ "I think **THE RIGHTEOUS** eight "**remained on the Earth**" and **ALL The Evil Doers** were taken away to Sheol.

3) Jesus said, "*That is how it will be when the Son of Man comes.*"

8) *At **that time** two men will be working in a field: **one will be taken away**, **the other will be left behind.***

A) Now **if Jesus** is telling us **The Truth**, and **I certainly will choose to believe Jesus**; He said that **one will be taken away;** in **Noah's day** only **the ~ "unrighteous" ~ was taken away.** And the others will be left behind. In **Noah's day the only ones "left behind"** were the **Saved or "Righteous" ones**.

9) Verse **45** tells of a faithful and wise servant who will feed His Sheep at the proper time. ~~~ I ~~~ wonder who that could be?

The Holy Spirit revealed to me that the **Word is The Father**, therefore **ONLY** The **Father knows** of Christ's return. Then God's Word will **reveal to us ALL about Christ's return.**

HISTORY'S GREATEST PROPHECY

History's Greatest Prophecy which is **Daniel 9:24 - 27**, refers to a time frame from about **1076 BC** ~ to **Christ's Second return**. It was approximately **1146 BC** when Jesus brought them out of the wilderness and gave them instructions to plant for six years then let the land rest on the seventh year. For the seventh year shall be a sabbatical. They were in the land for **490 years** and never let the land Rest. In that period of time of **490 years** the land should have rested **70 years**. Then Jesus allows them to be taken captive to Babylon to let the land rest for **70 years** all at one time.

Dan 12:9 *Daniel, go about your business, because the meaning of this* **message will remain secret** *until* **the end of time**. **(CEV)**

The following examination will take us through the process of why God's people were in Babylon for **70 years**. ~ Daniel now understands the reason they are there is because they disobeyed The **WORD** from God.

Daniel will receive ~ **"HISTORYS GREATEST PROPHECY!!!** ~ A time period from the ~ (**"_SIGNING_"**) ~ of a decree ~ till Jesus enters Jerusalem riding on a donkey on Palm Sunday will be **483** biblical years of **360** days each.

We will find that translates into **173,880 days**.
By the way ~ this number can be divided by
7 ~ **(173,880 divided by 7 = 24,840).**

We'll see why Jesus said, ~ And he answered and said unto them, "**I tell you** that, **if** these should hold their peace, the **stones** would immediately **cry out"**

Let's take a look at The **WORD**

Daniel 9:2 *In the first year of his reign I Daniel understood by books the number of the years, whereof the word of the LORD came to Jeremiah the prophet, that he would accomplish **seventy years** in the **desolations** of Jerusalem* **(KJV)**. ~

Daniel was reading the words that were spoken to Jeremiah in; **Jeremiah 29:10** *For thus saith the LORD, that after **seventy years** be accomplished at Babylon I will visit you, and perform my good word toward you, in causing you to return to this pla*ce **(RV)**. ~

Daniel is now convinced **why** they are in Babylon as he states in; **Daniel 9:10** *Neither have we obeyed the voice of the LORD our God, to walk in his laws, which he set before us by his servants the prophets.***(KJV)**

Daniel understood the reason they were in Babylon was **because** the children of Israel had **disobeyed** God by **not doing** what he had **told** them to do. After God had brought them out of the wilderness, and before they went into the promise land, God had given them **specific instructions** as outlined in; ~

Leviticus 25:1 *And the LORD spake unto Moses in mount Sinai, saying, {2} Speak unto the children of Israel, and say unto them, **When** ye come into the land which I give you, then shall the land **keep a Sabbath** unto the LORD. {3} Six years thou shalt sow thy field, and six years thou shalt prune thy vineyard, and gather in the fruit thereof; {4} But in the **seventh year** shall be a **Sabbath of rest** unto the **land**, a Sabbath for the LORD: thou shalt neither sow thy field, nor prune thy vineyard. {5} That which groweth of its own accord of thy harvest thou shalt not reap, neither gather the grapes of thy vine undressed: for it is a year of rest unto the land. {6} And the **Sabbath** of the land shall be meat for you; for thee, and for thy servant, and for thy maid, and for thy hired servant, and for thy stranger that sojourneth with thee* **(KJV)**.

Daniel **understood** that his people had been **in** the promise land for **490 years**, and had never observed **one** Sabbatical year to let the land rest. Therefore; **Daniel 9:11** *Yea, all Israel **have transgressed** thy law, even by departing, that they might **not obey** thy voice; therefore the **curse** is poured upon us, and the oath that is written in the law of Moses the servant of God, **because** we have **sinned** against him* **(KJV)**. ~

And **what** was that **curse**?

It is found in; **Leviticus 26:27-35** *And **if** ye will **not** for all this hearken unto me, but walk **contrary** unto me; {28} Then **I** will walk **contrary** unto **you** also in fury; and I, even I, will chastise you **seven times** for your sins. {29} And ye shall eat the flesh of your sons, and the flesh of your daughters shall ye eat. {30} And I will destroy your high places, and cut down your images, and cast your carcasses upon the carcasses of your idols, and my soul shall **abhor** you. {31} And **I will** make your cities waste, and bring your sanctuaries unto desolation, and I will not smell the savor of your sweet odors. {32} And I will bring the land* into **_desolation_**: and your enemies which dwell therein shall be **_astonished_** at it. {33} And I will scatter you among the heathen, and will draw out a **_sword_** **_after you_**: and your land shall be **_desolate_**, and your cities waste. {34} **_Then_** shall the **_land_** enjoy her **_Sabbaths,_** as long as it lieth desolate, and ye be in your enemies' land; even then shall the land rest, and enjoy her **_Sabbaths._** {35} As long as it lieth desolate it shall rest; because it **_did not rest_** in your **_Sabbaths,_** **_when_** ye dwelt upon it (**KJV**)

2 Chronicles 36:15-21
And the LORD God of their fathers **_sent to them_** by his **_messengers_**, rising up betimes, and sending; because he had compassion on his people, and on his dwelling place: {16} But **_they_** **_mocked_** the **_messengers of God_**, and **_despised his words_**, and **_misused_** his prophets, **_until_** the wrath of the LORD arose **_against_** his people, till there was no remedy.

{17} Therefore he brought upon them the king of the Chaldees, who **_slew_** their young men with the sword in the house of their sanctuary, and had **_no compassion_** upon young man or maiden, old man, or him that stooped for age: he gave them **_all_** into his hand. {18} And all the vessels of the house of God, great and small, and the treasures of the house of the LORD, and the treasures of the king, and of his princes; all these he **_brought to Babylon_**.

{19} And they burnt the house of God, and brake down the wall of Jerusalem, and burnt all the palaces thereof with fire, and destroyed all the goodly vessels thereof. {20} And them that had escaped from the sword carried he away to **_Babylon_**; where they were servants to him and his sons **_until_** the reign of the kingdom of Persia:

{21} To **_fulfill_** the word of the LORD by the mouth of Jeremiah, **_until_** the land had enjoyed her **_Sabbaths_**: for as long as she lay desolate she kept Sabbath, to fulfill **_threescore and ten_** **_years._** (**KJV**)

Chapter 32
~~~ GABRIEL ~ Gives Daniel ~ "The Seventy Week Prophecy ~~~

Daniel 9:24 **_Seventy_** weeks are determined upon thy people and upon thy holy city, **_to finish_** the transgression, and to make an end of **_sins,_** and to make **_reconciliation_** for iniquity, and to bring in **_everlasting righteousness_**, and to seal up the vision and **_prophecy_**, and to **_anoint_** the most Holy. (**KJV**)

Six things are outlined here;
        1) To finish the transgression,

2) To make an end of sins,
3) To make reconciliation for iniquity,
4) To bring in everlasting Righteousness,
5) To seal up the vision and the prophecy,
6) To anoint the most Holy.

Daniel 9:25 *Know therefore and **understand**, that ("**FROM**") the going forth of the **commandment** – (That is the signing of a document) ~ to restore and to build Jerusalem "**UNTO**" the Messiah the Prince **shall be** seven weeks, and threescore and two weeks: the street shall be built again, **and the wall**, even in troublous times* **(KJV)**.

The commandment that was given to restore and rebuild Jerusalem is **found** in; **Nehemiah 2:5-7** ~ *{5} And I said unto the king, If it please the king, and if thy servant have found favor in thy sight, that thou wouldest send me unto Judah, unto the city of my fathers' sepulchers, that I may **build it**. {6} And the king said unto me, (the queen also sitting by him,) For how long shall thy journey be? And when wilt thou return? So it pleased the king to send me; and I set him a time.*

*{7} Moreover I said unto the king, If it please the king, let **letters** be **given** ~ (*"**the signing of a document**")* ~ *me to the governors beyond the river, that they may convey me over till I come into Judah;* **(KJV)**

Attaxerxes Longimanus **signed papers** allowing Nehemiah to go and rebuild Jerusalem. God said: that day is the **starting** point of a (specific time period;) and ~ ("**from**") ~ that **day** "*until*" Jesus is declared the Messiah the Prince will be **483 years**.

$$7 \text{ weeks} = 7 \text{ years} \times 7 = 49 \text{ years } 49$$
$$+62 \text{ weeks} = 62 \text{ years} \times 7 = 434 \text{ years } +434$$
$$69 \text{ weeks} = 69 \text{ years} \times 7 = 483 \text{ years } = 483$$

A **biblical** year consists of **360 days**, so if you multiply **483** years x the **number**, of days in a year, which is 360 days and that is **483 x 360** = (**173,880**) days. This is **exactly** how many **days** it would be , **FROM** the **day** that Nehemiah got his papers **signed** UNTIL Jesus was to be **declared** the **Messiah** the **prince**.

Now turn to; **Luke 19:28-31** - *{28} And when he had thus spoken, he went before, **ascending up to Jerusalem.** {29} And it came to pass, when he was come nigh to Bethphage and Bethany, at the mount called the mount of Olives, he sent two of his disciples, {30} Saying,*

*Go ye into the village over against you; in the which at your entering ye shall **find a colt tied, whereon yet never man sat**: loose him, and bring him hither. {31} And if any man ask you, Why do ye loose him? thus shall ye say unto him, Because the Lord hath need of him* **(KJV)**.

Jesus was in the process of fulfilling scripture That Gabriel had Spoken to Daniel, as Jesus knew full well, and the Father had revealed this **Secret thing** that He was doing to whom **He had chosen**,

(Deut 29:29) ~ Because these few knew what was taking place, they in obedience were quoting;

Zechariah 9:9 *Rejoice greatly, O daughter of Zion; shout, O daughter of Jerusalem: behold, thy King **cometh unto** thee: he is just, and having **salvation;** lowly, and riding upon an ass, and upon a colt the foal of an ass* **(KJV)**.

Drop down to, **Luke 19:38-40** *{38} Saying, Blessed be the King that cometh in the name of the Lord: peace in heaven, and glory in the highest. {39} And some of the Pharisees from among the multitude said unto him, Master, **rebuke** thy disciples. {40} And he answered and said unto them, **I tell you** that, **if** these should hold their peace, the **stones** would immediately **cry out*** **(KJV)**.

Why did Jesus say that the **rocks** would **cry out**? Because this **was** the ~ ("**173,880th**") ~ day "**FROM**" the signing of the document to go and rebuild Jerusalem *UNTIL* the Messiah the Prince was **declared**, just **exactly** as God had **spoken** to Daniel by the Angel Gabriel. This was the **last day** of the **483 years** in exact fulfillment of prophecy.

In ~ **Luke 19:41** this was on palm Sunday that this day was being fulfilled.

Luke 19:41 *And when he was come near, he beheld the city, and wept over it, {42} Saying, If thou hadst known, even thou, at least in this thy day, the things which belong unto thy peace! but now they are hid from thine eyes.{43} For the days shall come upon thee, that thine enemies shall cast a trench about thee, and compass thee round, and keep thee in on every side,{44} And shall lay thee even with the ground, and thy children within thee; and they shall not leave in thee one stone upon another; because thou knewest not the time of thy visitation* **(KJV)**.

Daniel 9:26 *And after threescore and two weeks shall Messiah be **cut off**, but not for himself: and the people of the **prince that shall come shall destroy the city and the sanctuary**; and*

the end thereof shall be with a flood, and unto the end of the war desolations are determined.
(KJV)

After this time period of **483** years it says that the Messiah shall be **cut off**, that is a Jewish idiom that means **to be killed**; but not for himself, **he died for us**!

Now The "**Father**" ~ **(Jesus)** ~ said, that it would be **173,880** days from the time that Attaxerxes Longimanus ~ **(signed a Treaty)** ~ for allowing Nehemiah to go and rebuild Jerusalem and the walls, till Jesus was declared the Messiah, **The King**. ~

If The Father has Revealed that to us, inasmuch as the exactness that really happened; what are some of the odds that a mere man could predict such a thing in the first place.

The story that comes to mind concerning this matter, involves something like this. A man that worked for a company that predicted the odds for different companies or organizations such as the lotteries or gambling etc.; was asked to figure out the odds of a mere man predicting this kind of thing to the day including the multiplicity of the problem. This was his answer:

In fact as I remember, he couldn't figure this out by long hand methods, so he entered this information **into a computer**, and this was the report. The **computer printed** out this information:

~ It would take **1,000 "EARTHS"** covered with Silver Dollars eighteen inches deep; and you only have **one chance** to pick up the "**ONE Marked silver dollar**". ~

The Earth has about **5,490,000,000,000,000** square feet with about **51,000** silver dollars (**18 inches high**) per square foot. So One earth would need about **2,799,900,000,000,000,000,000,000,000** Silver Dollars to cover it eighteen inches deep, then the computer said that it would take *one thousand Earth* to get to the right number of Silver Dollars! So if you multiply that number by one thousand you come up with the odds of a mere man guessing these facts one time.

This number is **2,799,900,000,000,000,000,000,000,000,000**: ~
This is ONE chance in **Two Decillion 799 Nonillion 900 Octillion** to get it right!!!
Now if you can't see the *FATHER* in this equation, then maybe one has a problem.

This time period of **173,880** days is not something that "I" came up with. It was Sir Robert Anderson from England, I believe. This was His attempt to PROVE God's word **WRONG**; Which is **IMPOSSIBLE**. I understand he spent most of his life on research of **Dan 9:24-27**. I think, but not sure, that the title of his book was "**The Coming Prince**, by **Sir Robert Anderson** ".

Daniel 9:27 *And **he** shall **confirm** the **covenant** with many for **one week**: and in the **midst** of the week **he** shall cause the **sacrifice** and the oblation **to cease**, and for the overspreading of abominations he shall make it desolate, even **until** the consummation, and that determined shall be poured upon the desolate* (**KJV**).

He, refers to the prince that **shall come**, in verse 26. This is who Jesus **referred** to in **John 5:43**, *I am come in my **Father's name**, and ye receive me **not**: if **another** shall come in his **own name**, him ye **will** receive* (**KJV**). ~ He was **referring** to the **anti-Christ** .

The Jews were **not looking** for the **Son of God**, they are looking for a **peacemaker** and that is what they are **going** to receive; but in the **middle** of Daniel's **seventieth** week the **anti-Christ** breaks the treaty.

Jesus said that the ~ ("**signing of a decree** ") ~ to allow Nehemiah to return and **rebuild** Jerusalem **started** the **first** time period, and that **483 years** would pass **before** the messiah the prince would be **declared**, this **same** God is saying that **when** Israel ~ ("**signs a peace treaty"**) ~ with the **anti-Christ**, this ("**BEGINS"**) the final **time period** of Daniel's **seventieth week** which is **seven** biblical years of **360** days each.

Dan 12:9 *He answered, "Go on about your life Daniel. The **message is hidden**. It will be a* **secre***t* ~~~ *(***"until the time of the end."***)* ~ {**10**} *Many people will be made pure--they will make themselves clean. But evil people will continue to be evil. And those **wicked people** will **not understan**d these things, but the* **"wise"** *people will* **understand them.**

Daniel 12:11 *And **FROM** the time that the daily **sacrifice** shall be **taken away**, and the abomination that maketh desolate set up, there shall be a thousand two hundred and ninety **days*** (**KJV**).

Chapter 33
~~~ The Anti-Christ Signs the Final Treaty ~~~

That Starts the Final 7 Years of Daniel's Prophecy
That fulfills Christ' Second Return!

There is going to be **1290 days**, or **3 ½ years "FROM"** the time the **"peace treaty"** is "*signed*" "**UNTIL**" the daily "**sacrifice**" is taken away.

"**From**" the time the daily sacrifice is taken away, "**UNTIL**" the abomination that maketh desolate is set up will be **1290 days**, or **3 ½ years**.

Daniel 12:12 *Blessed is **he** that **waiteth**, and **cometh** to the thousand three hundred and five and thirty days.* **(KJV)**

This scripture gives a time period of **1335 days,** which is **45 days beyond** the time of the abomination that maketh desolate, and I believe that this is the days that Jesus referred to in ~

Matthew 24:15-22 *{15}When ye therefore shall see the **abomination** of **desolation**, spoken of by **Daniel** the **prophet,** stand in the **holy place,** (whoso readeth, let him **understand**:) {16} Then let them which be in Judea flee into the mountains: {17} Let him which is on the housetop not come down to take any thing out of his house: {18} Neither let him which is in the field return back to take his clothes. {19} And woe unto them that are with child, and to them that give suck in those days! {20} But pray ye that your flight be not in the winter, neither on the Sabbath day: {21} For then shall be **great tribulation**, such as **was not since** the **beginning** of the world **to this time**, no, nor **ever shall** be. {22} And except **those days** should be **shortened,** there should **no flesh** be saved: **but** for the **elect's** ~ (we are the **ELECT**) ~ sake those days **shall** be shortened* **(KJV)**.

This Great Tribulation that Jesus Refers to is going to take place after you see The **(Abomination of Desolation)** ~ Which is seven biblical years after the Anti-Christ signs "The Peace Treaty" ~ with Israel. Did you notice that ~ ({"**FOR THE ELECTS**"}) ~ sake those days **shall** be shortened ~ It is pretty inclusive that "**Christians are still Here**", according to Jesus.

Chapter 34
~~~ Jesus' Response Concerning HIS RETURN ~~~

Mat 24:3 *And as He was sitting on the Mount of Olives, the disciples came to Him privately, saying, "Tell us, when shall these things be? And what shall be the "**sign of Your coming**," and of **the end of the age?"** {4} And Jesus answered and said to them: "Take heed that ~*

~ "**no one** deceives you." ~ {5} For many will come in My name, saying, 'I am the Christ,' and **they will deceive many.** {6} And you will hear of wars and rumors of wars. See that you are not disturbed; for all these things must come to pass, but **the end is not yet**. {7} For nation shall rise up against nation, and kingdom against kingdom, and there will be famines, pestilences, and earthquakes in various places. {8} But all these things are the **beginning of sorrows. {9}** Then they will **hand you over to tribulation** and **they will kill you**, and **you will be hated by all nations, on account of My name.** {10} And **then many will fall away**, and **they will betray one another**, and **they will hate one another.** {11} Then many **false prophets will be raised up**, and **they will deceive many.** {12} And because **lawlessness will increase**, **the love of many will grow cold**. {13} But he who **endures to the "end"** shall be {14} And this good news of the kingdom will be proclaimed in all the world for a testimony to all the nations, and **then the end will come**. (EMTV) ~

15} "**Therefore** when you **see the "abomination of desolation**,"
spoken of **through Daniel the prophet**,
standing in the holy place"
(**whoever reads**,
let him understand) (**EMTV**).

Chapter 35
A Simple description of what the BIBLE is about!

1) The Bible is about –

    1) A King
    2) Who has a Kingdom
    3) And His Royal Family.

2) **The Bible is about –**

    1) God Who is Spirit
    2) His Kingdom which is Spiritual
    3) And His Kids who are Spiritual

3) The Bible is about –

    1) God Who never changes
    2) His Kingdom which is Eternal
    3) And His Kids who are in Rebellion

4) The Bible is about –

      1) A God of Love

      2) Who sent His Son

      3) To Redeem His rebellious children

5) The Bible is about –

      1) A God of Mercy

      2) Who is full of Grace

      3) Who has brought Redemption.

6) The Bible is about –

      1) God's Word

      2) And hearing of that Word

      3) And Faith to believe that Word

7) The Bible is about –

      1) Life & Death

      2) A God of Salvation

3) And Jesus the Resurrection

Chapter 36
~~~ (*WORD IS FATHER*) ~~~

    (LVB) 1 Corinthians 2:9 ~ 13 *That is what is meant by the Scriptures which say that no mere man has ever seen, heard or even imagined what wonderful things God has ready for those who love the Lord. {10}* **But** *we know about these things because God has sent **his Spirit to tell us**, and his Spirit searches out and shows us all of **God's deepest secrets**. {11} ~ No one can really know what anyone else is thinking, or what he is really like, except that person himself. And **no one can know God's thoughts** except God's **own** Spirit.{12} And God has actually <u>given us His Spirit</u> (<u>not</u> the <u>world's</u> spirit) to tell us about the wonderful **free** gifts of grace and blessing that God **has** given us.{13} ~ In telling you about these gifts we have even used the very words given to us **by the Holy Spirit,** not words that we as men might choose. So we use the Holy Spirit's **words** to explain the Holy Spirit's **facts**.* **(LVB)**

    The truth is, that unless you receive for yourself, the provision **God freely gives to anyone** that asks; which is "**The Gift of His Spirit**", it will be **impossible** for you to understand this book because it is **spiritually** discerned.

Chapter 37
Romans 10:8-11

Romans 10:8 *For **salvation** that comes **from** trusting Christ ~ which is what we preach ~ is already within **easy reach** of each of us; in fact, it is as near as our own hearts and **mouths.** {9} For if you **tell others** with your **own mouth** that Jesus Christ is **your Lord**, and believe in your own heart that God has raised him from the dead, **you will be saved**. {10} For it is **by** believing in his heart that a man becomes right **with** God; and with his **mouth he tells others** of his faith, **confirming** his salvation. {11} For the Scriptures tell us that no one who **believes in Christ** will ever be disappointed.(LVB)*

So why not receive "The Gift" of **salvation now** - Pray this simple prayer: Lord I know **how** I am, and that I certainly am not **doing** things your way. I am **asking** for your help, will you come **into** my life and lead me into **doing** things **your** way. I **receive** you now and thank you for ,**"The Free Gift of Your Salvation"** in Jesus' Name Amen!!!

Chapter 38
~~~ My Prayer ~~~

Father ~ I pray that you would give unto us the wisdom to, really understand who Christ is and all that He bas done for us. I pray that you will flood our hearts with your light that, we might be able to comprehend with the rest of the saints, the glorious future that you want to share with us.

Father we all can remember that we were lost without your son, being aliens from the commonwealth of Israel; strangers **from** the covenants of promise, having **no hope**, without you in this world. But today we are thankful that **through** the Shed Blood of Your Son, and the **receiving** of Him, you **have** translated us out of Satan's kingdom and **back** into yours. We are eternally grateful and thankful that we are no more strangers and foreigners but **fellowcitizens** with the **Saints**, and are **now** of the household of God.

Father we thank you that we **have** received the ***Resurrected*** Spirit of your Son, that old things are passed away, and all thing **have** become new. We thank you that the ***Body of sin*** has been ***destroyed***, the old man ***has been*** crucified, and that we no longer have to serve sin!

We thank you that we **now** live by the Faith of your dear son who has **circumcised our hearts** and *has* made us like unto the **Angels of God**. Father we thank you that you said, Moses my servant is dead and commanded Joshua to lead the people **into** the Promised land, by that comparison, you are going to **do away** with the **doctrines of men** and teaching us by

your Spirit the **Meat** of the Word; which is understanding **by** Spirit **what you meant** by what you have said.

Father I thank you now for the anointing of your Spirit that abides within me that no **man** had to teach me the things that I speak, for it is only **you** that **knoweth** all things and truly **no man** can **receive** anything **except** it be given to him **from** heaven, for you have said, "**that it is not by might, nor by power, but by your Spirit;** In Jesus Name Amen!

Grace And Peace To All,
by Ronald Dyer

www.ingramcontent.com/pod-product-compliance
Lightning Source LLC
Chambersburg PA
CBHW081406280526
45788CB00009B/3000